SECOND-HAND KNOWLEDGE

RECENT TITLES IN CONTRIBUTIONS IN LIBRARIANSHIP
AND INFORMATION SCIENCE
SERIES EDITOR: PAUL WASSERMAN

Defending Intellectual Freedom: The Library and the Censor
Eli M. Oboler

Management for Librarians: Fundamentals and Issues
John R. Rizzo

Corporate Authorship: Its Role in Library Cataloging
Michael Carpenter

Librarians and Labor Relations: Employment Under Union Contracts
Robert C. O'Reilly and Marjorie I. O'Reilly

Reading Research and Librarianship: A History and Analysis
Stephen Karetzky

Teaching Library Use: A Guide for Library Instruction
James Rice, Jr.

The Public Librarian as Adult Learners' Advisor: An Innovation in
Human Services
Jane A. Reilly

Illustrative Computer Programming for Libraries:
Selected Examples for Information Specialists
Charles H. Davis and Gerald W. Lundeen

Micropublishing: A History of Scholarly Micropublishing
in America, 1938-1980
Alan Marshall Meckler

Stereotype and Status: Librarians in
the United States
Pauline Wilson

The Client-Centered Academic Library:
An Organizational Model
Charles R. Martell, Jr.

Public Library User Fees: The Use and
Finance of Public Libraries
Nancy A. Van House

SECOND-HAND KNOWLEDGE

AN INQUIRY INTO COGNITIVE AUTHORITY

Patrick Wilson

Contributions in Librarianship and
Information Science, Number 44

Greenwood Press
Westport, Connecticut ● London, England

Library of Congress Cataloging in Publication Data

Wilson, Patrick, 1927-
  Second-hand knowledge.

  (Contributions in librarianship and information
science, ISSN 0084-9243 ; no. 44)
  Includes bibliographical references and index.
  1. Knowledge, Sociology of.   2. Libraries.
3. Information science.   I. Title.   II. Series.
BD175.W55   1983   306'.42   82-21069
ISBN 0-313-23763-8 (lib. bdg.)

Library of Congress Catalog Card Number: 82-21069
ISBN: 0-313-23763-8
ISSN: 0084-9243

First published in 1983

Greenwood Press
A division of Congressional Information Service, Inc.
88 Post Road West
Westport, Connecticut 06881

Printed in the United States of America

P

CONTENTS

PREFACE

This book had its origin in a nagging concern about the apparent unconcern of librarians and information scientists for the difference between information and misinformation, joined with the apparent assumption that libraries are simply storehouses of knowledge, and the literature of science and scholarship simply the written record of the continual production of knowledge. How could one account for the strange unconcern? Was the assumption perhaps not so naive as it seemed? Satisfactory answers to these questions turned out to require looking not just at librarians and information scientists but at almost everyone else too: at those who claim to have or to produce specialized knowledge and at all those faced with the question of whose claims to believe. What was needed was a general examination of the phenomena of cognitive authority and the production of knowledge before addressing the particular situation of the information professional.

Although knowledge is its central concern, this work is not one of philosophical epistemology; philosophers will quickly see that I am not addressing their questions.[1] This is, rather, a work of social epistemology. Social epistemology presumably is what the sociology of knowledge is about, but sociologists have no monopoly on the subject. The phrase *social epistemology* was used thirty years ago by Egan and Shera to refer to study of the production, distribution, and utilization of intellectual products.[2] It is highly appropriate that the phrase should have been introduced in an essay on the theory of bibliography, for the reflective bibliographer is naturally interested in the ways in which graphic records emerge out of the attempt to increase knowledge and enter into its dissemination and utilization. Any study of these subjects leads quickly to questions of cognitive authority, or would be halfhearted and incomplete if it did not.

A writing about knowledge is likely to raise questions about whether what it says applies to itself, and I am aware that this book raises such questions. It is at several points an example of what it is talking about; I will let others decide where those points are.

Part of chapter 4 derives from a paper I gave at the Fortieth Conference of the Graduate Library School, University of Chicago, and published in *Library Quarterly* 50 (1980): 4-21, © 1980 by the University of Chicago. I am indebted to Michael Buckland, Elfreda Chatman, William S. Cooper, M. E. Maron, and Pauline Wilson for helpful comments on drafts of various parts of this work; to Mona Farid, Betsy Flores, Irene Linning, and Godelieve Scott for research assistance at various times; to Michael Cooper and Nancy Van House for helpful discussions; to Dorothy Koenig for useful bibliographical references; and to Genevieve McNeil for expeditious typing of the manuscript.

Notes

1. However, see the last paragraph of the Bibliographical Essay at the end of this work.

2. Margaret E. Egan and Jesse H. Shera, "Foundations of a Theory of Bibliography," *Library Quarterly* 22 (1952): 125-37. Shera says that Egan coined the phrase: Jesse H. Shera, *The Foundations of Education for Librarianship* (New York: Becker and Hayes, 1972), p. 112.

SECOND-HAND
KNOWLEDGE

1 FIRST-HAND AND SECOND-HAND KNOWLEDGE

Perspectives

Our talk about what we think and what we learn is pervaded by metaphors, especially spatial and visual ones. We make points, take lines, occupy positions; we have views, we see others' points, but from our own angle of vision. Seeing stands for understanding and for learning in general: the way things look to me, from my point of view, from where I stand, is the way I understand things to be. Mental life is an affair of seeing and standing—and of sitting, for as people say, where you stand depends on where you sit, at least in bureaucratic circles. It is also, almost obsessively, an affair of perspective: your perspective differs from mine, narrow perspectives differ from wide ones, partial from comprehensive ones, insiders' perspectives from outsiders'.[1]

There is a difference in emphasis conveyed by the spatial and the visual metaphors. Positions and standpoints, along with points and lines, suggest location in an imaginary space of ideas, while perspectives and points of view suggest both location and what one sees from the location or how things look from the location. Sometimes when we talk metaphorically, there is available a solid literal alternative way of talking, and the metaphors are used just for stylistic reasons—to give variety and vivacity to talk. But when we talk of the mind, the metaphors are not easily replaceable by nonmetaphorical terms. The metaphors are really almost our basic vocabulary for talk about thinking and learning. It is especially hard to eliminate talk of perspectives in favor of nonmetaphorical alternatives. There is no particular reason to want to do so if the perspectival talk is understandable. But it is good occasionally to explore our metaphors because they can mislead us. One linguist has made a persuasive case that much careful as well as casual thought and talk about human communication is warped by a faulty basic metaphor, and perhaps our thoughts about thought are also warped by pervasive but faulty metaphors.[2]

Let us look closely at the metaphor of perspective. The place to start is with the most literal case of perspective: visual perspective. The basic facts about visual perspective are these. First, what you can see, what will appear in your field of vision, depends on where you are and in what direction you are looking. Second, apparent size diminishes with distance; the farther away an object is, the smaller it looks. Third, you cannot see around corners; you see the front of a thing, but not its back or its insides. Fourth, angular relationships vary with position in the visual field. A square object looked at from an angle does not look quite square and looks less so the greater the angle between it and the viewer. We can take these as the most important facts about visual perspective.

Now let us ask how well the perspectival metaphor fits social experience, our direct involvement with the world of human thought and action. Are there analogous rules of social perception? So it seems, and quite striking analogies too. First consider the relation of apparent size and distance. The closer we are to some feature of social life, the bigger it seems to us—bigger in the sense of importance, salience, significance, bigger in the sense that it occupies a larger share of attention, effort, interest, reflection. My family, my job, my friends, my school, my town: these are big; or they naturally seem bigger to me than your family, your job, and so on. By an effort I may manage to correct for this natural illusion of size, but it does not come easily, and we are all familiar with people who absurdly overestimate not only their own importance but the importance of the things they are personally involved with. We all are egocentric and have to learn to correct for the illusions of social perception due to egocentrism. But it is doubtful that we succeed very well. Evidence of failure is everywhere. It appears, for instance, as the aggrandizement effect, "a tendency for group members to assign unrealistically high ratings to their own groups in comparison with competing groups," to think one's own school among the leading schools, one's own business among the leading businesses, and so on.[3] Apparent size varies not only with social distance but with temporal distance too. Events seem smaller the more remote they are in time. We sometimes say to ourselves that we are too close to events or situations to see them in their proper perspective and expect the passage of time to put enough distance between us and them to see them properly. The variation of apparent size with distance surely qualifies as one of the basic facts about human experience.

The corner rule applies too in a way. We encounter only the "front" that others present to us. Social encounters are managed so that each party sees only what the other permits. The dramatological view of social relations is based on the corner rule. The angular distortion rule seems to apply as well: your view of the situation differs from mine because though we are both involved, I am centrally involved and you are peripherally involved, or a bystander. What is central and what is a side issue is a matter of the angle from which one approaches it. What one faces directly and what one encounters only by witnessing from the sidelines depends on the angle of one's involvement.

Most important is the basic rule that what we can experience of the social world depends on our social location: our location in time and in space and in the network of social relationships. Whom I will encounter and what the encounter will be like depend on who and where I am: a middle-aged academic in northern California in the late twentieth century, a penniless Scottish immigrant in New York in the late nineteenth century. As we move from one social location to another, the range and character of experience change accordingly. Moving from the bottom of the heap to the top, or conversely, or from one social circle to another, we move from one range of experience to a very different one. All in all, the perspectival metaphor seems strikingly appropriate for social experience.

Lenses

It is not so clear that the perspectival metaphor works as well in other contexts in which it is frequently employed. People talk of the Marxist perspective, the clinician's perspective, the "early symbolic-interaction perspective," the Catholic perspective, different perspectives on personality, the sociological perspective, and so on. The world as seen from the perspective of an economist looks different from the world as seen from the perspective of a psychologist; the Christian's perspective differs from the atheist's. Such talk is familiar, but it may be misleading, for these perspectives are actually baggage one carries from one social location to another. They condition not what sorts of encounters one will have, but what one will notice in them and how one will interpret them. There is another familiar metaphor that fits better. Rosa Luxemburg complained that Eduard Bernstein, having spent too much time in England, saw the world through English spectacles.[4] That is, he had acquired English ways of thinking. The concepts and theories and habitual modes of thought one carries around will determine how the world looks and what one makes of what one sees, as much as will the social location from which one views the world.

Concepts and theories constitute a sort of lens through which we look at the world.[5] If the Marxist perspective differs from others, it is because of a difference in the conceptual and theoretical apparatus employed to interpret experience, not because of a difference in location. And if we forget this, we are likely inadvertently to make a serious mistake. Different visual and social perspectives are not in conflict with each other even though what things look like from different perspectives differs enormously. Moving from one social location to another, one will see different things with varying apparent sizes and appearances, but these are just different aspects or sides of the whole complex of social life, and the more aspects or sides one can see, the better one's view of the world. The way the world really is might be thought of as the sum of the ways it looks from all possible locations, but it cannot be thought of as the sum of the ways it appears when viewed with all possible sorts of conceptual and theoretical apparatus, all possible theoretical lenses. Many of those lenses give inaccurate as well as distorted pictures of the world. They lead one to think one is seeing things that are not there, and they prevent one from seeing things that are there. There are certainly mistakes of judgment to which we are prone simply by virtue of the laws of social perspective. The egocentric illusion of apparent size is the most obvious. We can at least partly overcome those illusions without giving up having experience entirely. But the mistakes of judgment to which we are led by bad theories and inapplicable concepts have to be overcome by giving up the theories and concepts. We have to discard the faulty lenses for better ones.

We have to beware thinking that all the different partial perspectives provided by different conceptual approaches to the world can somehow be coordinated and merged to arrive at a single, consistent, total view of the world. There are certainly many different conceptual and theoretical approaches to the world that are mutually consistent though they provide different pictures. What an economist sees is likely to differ from what a sociologist sees, but we may be able easily enough to add them together to get a more complete view. But there are plenty of approaches that give results that cannot be added together; they give pictures that are not pictures of this world at all. The perspectival metaphor is likely to lead us to underestimate or play down conceptual conflict; "you and I have different views, but that's all right; it's simply a difference in point of view and no doubt we're each right in our own ways." That would be fair enough if our conceptual schemes were the same or at least consistent with each other but not if they are not.

If concepts and theories are metaphorically lenses through which one sees the world, is there anything corresponding to sight without glasses? We put on spectacles to correct our vision, but the wrong pair of glasses can make things worse. Sight without glasses must be simply use of common sense. A person must always have some theoretical approach to experience, some conceptual framework, just as he must always occupy some social location or another. Experience is inconceivable apart from both. Common sense is simply one's basic supply of notions of what the world is like—what kinds of things there are, how they work, how one can learn about them. A basic metaphysics and epistemology are parts of everyone's mental furniture. The name for them is common sense. As the anthropologist Clifford Geertz says, common sense is a theory of the world—a thin theory but nevertheless a theory.[6] Of course, there is not just a single commonsense theory of the world; what is common sense to one group is madness to another. But common sense, whatever its content in a particular case, does represent the "natural" conceptual approach to the world. Unaided common sense can be helped by appropriate conceptual and theoretical apparatus that, as lenses or spectacles, extend the range of perception and improve its acuity; it can also be hindered by distorting lenses.

The View From The Top

In one respect the metaphor of perspective is misleading when applied to social experience. As I move away in space from a particular point, objects seem smaller and smaller, but I can also see a wider and wider area. As I move up into space, the cities and towns look smaller and smaller, but I can see more of the world until, on a spaceship headed for the moon, I can see the whole planet (though only one side of it and only the outside). Our perspective or field of vision widens. We come closer to seeing objects in their true proportions as we see the things we were previously close to in the context of a larger range of territory. Now do we not do the same in social perception? As we move away from a social situation, does it not only seem smaller but also part of a wider field? Not really. Social encounters and social perception are short-range phenomena. The visual analogy would hold if there were a limit, say ten feet, to the distance beyond which we could not see an object at all, even in the best light. Except for the crucially important possibility of long-range communication by mail or telephone, when we leave a situation, we are no longer experiencing what we did when in the situation, only in an attenuated way. We cease to have those experiences at all. We may come back for a visit from time to time and others may report to us what is going on, but it is now outside the range of our personal experience. Others' reports are a pale substitute for being there ourselves, as others' reports of what they can see but we cannot are only a pale substitute for seeing, even at a great distance. The perspectival metaphor fails at a crucial point.

All of this goes against common notions. When we move up in a hierarchy, from clerk to district manager to chairman of the board of directors, is there not a sense in which we move to a position from which we can, and are indeed obligated to, see the big picture? And as we move away from events in time, is it not true that we can see an entire large pattern of events better than we can when we are in the middle of them? Is this not the advantage of the historian over the journalist? And does not the detached spectator think he is better able than those caught up in the excitement of active participation in a political campaign to see the campaign in its proper perspective? No. The right way to describe the situation is to say that the director, the historian, the detached spectator deliberately construct pictures of the situation, trying to include significant features while omitting insignificant ones, trying to give each feature its proper share of space.

The picture is constructed from materials provided by others' reports and observations, as well as by one's own direct experience, and memories of previous occurrences. The detached spectator is not simply spectating; he is painting a picture, constructing a representation, which he works over, erasing this part and adding that, enlarging this feature and diminishing that, as he revises his notions of proper proportion in the light of his readings of the reports that reach him. The farther he is from the scene, the more he has to rely on reports from others, and the less his experience can guide him in preparing his picture. The view from the top is not a view seen from the top but a picture drawn from the vantage point of responsibility (perhaps self-imposed) for getting a good picture of a large scene, based in part on what one has oneself observed and in part on what others tell one. The larger the scene to be depicted, the more one has to rely on what others tell one. The view from the top is a picture drawn largely at second-hand; we can paint a picture of the world as it looks from ten thousand miles up that is based entirely on what we ourselves see, but our pictures of the social world have to be based on hearsay if they are to be big pictures.

Experientia Docet?

Experience teaches, but not much.[7] Most of us go through life occupying a narrow range of social locations. If all we could know of the world was what we could find out on the basis of first-hand experience, we would know little. But what we can find out from first-hand experience itself depends crucially on the stock of ideas we bring to the interpretation and understanding of our encounters with the world. If we had to depend entirely on ideas that we ourselves invented, we would make little sense of the world. We mostly depend on others for ideas, as well as for information about things outside the range of direct experience. Others supply us with new theoretical perspectives as well as with information from other social perspectives. Much of what we think about the world is what we have second hand from others. The phrase *second hand* is especially appropriate in suggesting second best, not so good as first hand; for in an obvious way, finding out by being told differs from finding out by seeing or hearing or living through an experience.[8] Being told about a piece of music is no substitute for hearing it, reading about being in love is no substitute for being in love, and in general, the more remote anything told us is from our own experience, the thinner, more abstract, and purely verbal it is. Since there are plenty of experiences we would like to avoid having, the thinness of a merely verbal description is often not to be lamented. Second best is quite good enough. But elsewhere, verbal reports are not quite satisfactory substitutes for first-hand doing and observing. Yet we have to make do with them if we are to transcend the limits of personal experience.

What leads us to seek second-hand knowledge, and to whom are we led? Necessity is part of the answer to the first; "to those whom we think know something we do not know" is the short answer to the second. But what explains the fact that different people seem to need such different kinds and amounts of second-hand knowledge, and the fact that different people seem to have such different notions of who the people are from whom they can learn? We have to explore not what is known about the world, but rather what people think about knowledge—how they decide who knows what about what. That is a question about cognitive authority.

Notes

1. See Robert K. Merton, "Insiders and Outsiders: A Chapter in the Sociology of Knowledge," *American Journal of Sociology* 78 (1972): 9-47;

and Karl Mannheim, *Ideology and Utopia: An Introduction to the Sociology of Knowledge*, trans. Louis Wirth and Edward Shils (London: Kegan Paul, 1936). The historian Peter Gay calls the perspectivist view "the stock in trade of historiography, which justifies its existence with the argument that historians are doomed to limited perspectives." See his *Style in History* (New York: Basic Books, 1974), p. 197. For one of many of the discussions of perspectivism, see Gene Wise, *American Historical Explanations* (Homewood, Ill.: Dorsey Press, 1973), pp. 36-53.

2. Michael J. Reddy, "The Conduit Metaphor--A Case of Frame Conflict in Our Language about Language," in *Metaphor and Thought*, ed. Andrew Ortony (Cambridge: Cambridge University Press, 1979), pp. 284-324.

3. Theodore Caplow and Reece J. McGee, *The Academic Marketplace* (Garden City, N.Y.: Doubleday, Anchor Books, 1965), p. 37. Amusing confirmation is found in Frank R. Westie, "Academic Expectations for Professional Immortality: A Study of Legitimation," *Sociological Focus* 5 (1972): 1-25.

4. David McLellan, *Marxism after Marx: An Introduction* (London: Macmillan, 1979), p. 23.

5. Use of this metaphor is found everywhere. See, for instance, Oscar Handlin, *Truth in History* (Cambridge, Mass.: Belknap Press of Harvard University Press, 1979), p. 1: "The scholar's vision is subjective, at least to the extent that his own point of observation and the complex lenses of prejudice, interest, and preconception shape what he discerns and therefore what he can portray."

6. Clifford Geertz, "Common Sense as a Cultural System," *Antioch Review* 33 (Spring 1975): 5-26.

7. See Berndt Brehmer, "In One Word: Not from Experience," *Acta Psychologica* 45 (1980): 223-41, for a fascinating discussion of failures to learn from experience.

8. Good discussion of this is Jerome S. Bruner and David R. Olson, "Learning through Experience and Learning through Media," in *Communication Technology and Social Policy*, ed. George Gerbner et al. (New York: Wiley, 1973), pp. 209-27.

2   COGNITIVE AUTHORITY

Authority, Influence, Credibility

All I know of the world beyond the narrow range of my own personal experience is what others have told me. It is all hearsay. But I do not count all hearsay as equally reliable. Some people know what they are talking about, others do not. Those who do are my cognitive authorities.

It is tempting to avoid using the word *authority* entirely when talking of the relation between a person and those others from whom he thinks he can learn. The very mention of authority is likely to produce strong emotions, usually hostile. But *cognitive authority* is the right name for the phenomenon we want to explain. The best alternative is *epistemic authority*, which is no less offensive.[1] Passions may be dampened by realizing that what is at issue is not whether those who claim authority actually deserve it but simply what cognitive authority is and on what basis people do recognize it.

It is easier to start by talking of people as abstract A's and B's. We shall say that person A is a cognitive authority for person B with respect to sphere of interest S to the degree that what A says about questions falling within the sphere S carries weight for B. A is a cognitive authority for me in matters of politics to the degree that what A says about political questions carries weight with me. If what A says carries a lot of weight, he has a lot of authority: if it carries no weight, he has no authority.[2]

The first point to notice is that authority is a relationship involving at least two people. No one can be an authority all by himself; there has to be someone else for whom he is an authority. Having authority is thus different from being an expert, for one can be an expert even though no one else realizes or recognizes that one is, and even if one were the last person on earth. The second point to notice is that cognitive authority is a matter of degree; one can have a little of it or a lot. The third is that it is relative to a sphere of interest. On some questions, one may speak with authority; on other sorts of questions one might speak with none at all. A person might be an authority for many people but in different degrees or in different spheres. What A says about politics might carry great weight with me and a few others; what he says about religion might carry considerable weight with others, who ignore what he says about politics. If we speak about the authorities on a subject, we might mean either those whom everyone recognizes as cognitive authorities on the subject or those whom we recognize and whom everyone else ought to recognize, whether or not they actually do. It is one thing to find out who is recognized as an authority, quite another to decide that he ought or ought not to be recognized. The second is the question on which passions are aroused.

Cognitive authority is curiously different from the other familiar kind of authority, that of the person who is in a position to tell others what to do. Administrative authority, as we can call it, involves a recognized right to command others, within certain prescribed limits.[3] But the world's leading authority on butterflies, say, has no power to command. He cannot tell people what to think. One can acquire administrative authority by being appointed or elected to a position, but one cannot be appointed or elected the world's leading authority on butterflies, nor can one acquire that status by conquest or inheritance. Rather, cognitive authority is a kind of influence. Those who are my cognitive authorities are among those who influence my thinking.[4] Others who are not cognitive authorities may also influence me. The difference between them and the cognitive authorities is that I recognize the latter's influence as proper and the former's as not proper. Advertisements on television may influence my thoughts about which products are best or which political candidates deserve my vote. If I knew this was happening, I would try to counteract this effect, for I do not think they should be allowed to influence on my thinking.[5] The person whom I recognize as having cognitive authority is one whom I think should be allowed to have influence on my thinking, for I suppose he has a good basis for saying what he does. Whether he does explain to me why he thinks as he does or how he knows what he claims, I suppose that he could do this, and that whether or not I could follow him perfectly, his story would be satisfactory.

Cognitive authority is influence on one's thoughts that one would consciously recognize as proper. The weight carried by the words is simply the legitimate influence they have. Since we are only imperfectly aware of the ways and the degrees to which what others say influences our thoughts, we are likely to be unaware of the degrees of others' cognitive influence over us and hence of their authority. If we did know, we might feel that we were influenced less or more than we should be. If we lose faith in one of our authorities, he ceases to fill this role as we cease to believe that he has a good basis for saying what he does. He might continue to have an influence on us, but it would be one we would, if we realized the fact, think improper.

Cognitive authority is clearly related to credibility.The authority's influence on us is thought proper because he is thought credible, worthy of belief. The notion of credibility has two main components: competence and trustworthiness. A person is trustworthy if he is honest, careful in what he says, and disinclined to deceive. A person is competent in some area of observation or investigation if he is able to observe accurately or investigate successfully. In common sense and in a court of law, we distinguish between the ordinary competence of the average person and the special competence of the expert. There is a range of events and situations that we expect that any person of sound mind and normal faculties could report on correctly, matters in which we are all roughly equally competent observers and reporters because they require no special skill or knowledge to arrive at a correct description. This is the basis of ordinary social life. We are largely able to go on the assumption that our friends, neighbors, and work associates are generally trustworthy and of at least ordinary competence so that we can believe what they report of their own experience.[6] Insofar as we do make this assumption, we recognize these people as cognitive authorities in the sphere of their own experience, on matters they have been in a position to observe or undergo. (There may be some who would prefer not to speak of cognitive authority in this kind of case, but it is hard to see why one should not.) But we also recognize some people as having more than ordinary competence in particular spheres, and the spheres within which we think them competent are those in which they might come to have cognitive authority. Our cognitive authorities are clearly among those we think credible sources, but we might recognize someone as credible in an area even though he did not in fact have any influence on our thoughts. Those we think credible constitute the potential pool of cognitive authorities on which we might draw.

Knowledge and Opinion

What is the nature of the special competence that we attribute to whose whom we recognize as cognitive authorities? We naturally say that they are people whom we think know more than others. It is not a question of intelligence. A person of quite ordinary intelligence may have a special competence that we recognize as giving his words great weight. Neither is it a question of a stock of information. Significantly, in a classic treatise on the law of evidence, the expert is described as one especially fitted to acquire knowledge on the matter he speaks about.[7] It is not enough that he already have knowledge. This is understandable, for the point of introducing expert testimony into a trial is not to learn some body of previously accumulated knowledge but to get opinion on a new question arising in a particular case. The special competence that justifies cognitive authority amounts to more than a good and well-stocked memory. But what more?

It will help if we reflect on the old commonsense distinction between knowledge and opinion. This is the distinction between questions that have been settled beyond a doubt and questions on which doubt remains: between closed and open questions. The distinction is rough and practical, not subtle and speculative. There are hosts of questions that for the ordinary purposes of ordinary life we count as settled for all practical purposes: things we cannot seriously doubt, matters in which doubt seems capricious or abnormal. Epistemologists may debate endlessly whether we really do know the things we claim to know, the things we think have been settled beyond a doubt. That we can and do have a large stock of beliefs that we treat as closed questions is obvious. A question that is closed at one time may, of course, open up at another time; closure is not necessarily a permanent condition, and although we may be quite sure that a question will stay closed forever, we can easily be mistaken. What was a matter of knowledge may come to be a matter of opinion.

Whether a question is closed may itself be a closed question, but it may also be wide open. One group of people contends that the correctness of the theory of evolution, at least in general outline, has been established; its correctness is a closed question for them. Another group believes that it is very much an open question. The latter will hold that it is a matter of opinion whether the theory of evolution is correct; the former will hold that it is a matter not of opinion but of knowledge. It is precisely on this sort of question that we may consult our cognitive authorities. We want to know the status of a question: whether it is open or closed, settled or unsettled. The cognitive authority may have an answer. We can, if we like, treat this as knowledge about knowledge: the authority is one who knows about the status of questions within his sphere. Or we can, and this seems preferable, treat this as a matter of cognitive posture, as if expressed this way: "The appropriate stance to take is to treat this as a closed question to which the answer is such and such." Taken in that way, then, the cognitive authority's competence consists not only in being able to give us information about the world (first-level information) but in being able to advise us on how we should treat certain pieces of information.

If a question is open, there may be few or many competing and currently available answers, all of which will have the status of opinion. An opinion may be "almost knowledge"—the question being almost closed, one opinion having very strong support, almost enough to settle the question. If we treat a question as open, we next want to know the status of the various competing answers. Which is best? Are they evenly matched? Can any be ignored completely? Here too, different individuals and groups will have different answers, strenuously arguing the merits of their own view and denigrating those of others. In this sort of situation, we turn to our cognitive authorities for advice on which opinion to prefer or what attitude to take toward several competing opinions. Again we can treat this as knowledge about knowledge, and the authority as one who has second-order knowledge about the merits and defects, strengths and weaknesses, of opinions on an open question. Or, better, we may treat it as a matter of cognitive posture, and the ability to give good advice on what should be our stance toward the competing opinions. Taken in this way, we seek advice about a practical attitude, which might be expressed this way: "The best thing to do is to take this opinion as so well supported as to amount almost to knowledge, and ignore the others," or "The best thing to do is to treat them all as speculative and unfounded."

The cognitive authority is one to whom we turn for information but also one to whom we turn for advice, even (or particularly) in cases where it is clear that there is no knowledge to be had at all. Cognitive authorities are valued not just for their stocks of knowledge (answers to closed questions) but for their opinions (answers to open questions) and for their advice on the proper attitude or stance on questions and their proposed answers. Cognitive authority is not limited to the provision of knowledge or information, stopping when the limits of available knowledge are reached. Cognitive authority can extend to any sort of question: moral, religious, political, aesthetic, technical, scientific, philosophical—and be exercised in areas where all questions are open and expected to remain open indefinitely. Cognitive authority can extend over any province of thought, and although the authority cannot tell us what to think, he can influence us as in any other belief or attitude.

Degrees of Authority

The weight that one of my authorities' words carry for me might be so great as to settle questions for me. That he says this is so is enough to close the question. An absolute authority in a given sphere would be one whose answers to questions within that area were always taken as settling the question. This is the limiting case, not the ordinary case. Perhaps the hostility that many people feel toward the idea of authority in matters of thought comes from the notion that authority must be either absolute or nonexistent. But everyone takes other people's opinions and advice with different degrees of seriousness, depending on who the people are, and the essence of cognitive authority is simply that: taking people's opinions and advice more or less seriously. A cognitive egalitarian might hold that on some matters, or even on all matters, everybody's word should carry equal weight; in practice no one acts as if he thought this. Instead everyone recognizes others as unequal in judgment, even if equal in voting power. A cognitive nihilist might hold that no one's word should carry any weight, that we should never admit any influence of others on our thoughts as proper. In practice it would be hard to find many cognitive nihilists. We do trust others in varying degrees; we rely more or less heavily on other people as sources of information and advice, and the phenomenon of cognitive authority is just as real for those who recognize no absolute authorities as for those (if there are any) who recognize only absolute authorities.

Spheres of Authority

Authority is limited to spheres. On questions falling within the sphere, one speaks with authority, but on questions outside it, one may speak with no authority at all. But spheres of authority cannot always be defined precisely. We must not expect to find a neat geography of authority, with different individuals occupying well-specified areas. Some spheres of authority undoubtedly are fairly well defined, others exceedingly ill defined. The difference between a specialist and a generalist is a difference between more and less well-defined and circumscribed spheres of authority. But even when the specialist can define quite sharply a sphere within which he claims expertise, his authority may in fact extend well beyond that area, with diminishing degrees.

The well-defined sphere is actually a core area in which authority is at a maximum, surrounded by a penumbral area in which authority holds, but in smaller degrees. It is common for specialists to explain to others that the questions being put to them fall outside their area of expertise, a situation in which others are prepared to give a weight to their words that the specialist thinks they should not give. But although the specialist can define his own area of expertise, he cannot define his own sphere of authority; that is for others to do, with his help. Spheres of authority can be negotiated. The specialist offers to speak for the record on a certain range of matters, his audience urges him to widen the range, the specialist reluctantly agrees, and so on until no further adjustments are conceded. Or in the opposite situation, the specialist bluffly declares himself ready to speak on a broad range of matters; the audience tries to persuade him to confine his remarks to a narrower range. It is finally for the audience to decide on the scope of the sphere within which it would value the authority's words.

There are exceptions to this general rule. In what may be the extreme case, the authority is the one granted the right to define his own sphere of authority. This is the situation for one who believes in the authority.[8] Belief in is, or essentially involves, trust in the other, and trust may be so complete that one says, "Tell me what it is you know about; I trust you not to claim anything you do not possess." One who comes to believe in a religious leader, a prophet, a political messiah, may willingly and eagerly submit to the will of the leader and ask to be supplied with a definition of the sphere within which the leader wishes to be taken as authoritative. The highest degree of authority is likely to be authority that is in this way self-defining, authority that extends to the question of the scope of the sphere of authority itself.

We might recognize a person as an authority on everything: a universal authority. Perhaps children at some stage think their parents know everything; they take them to be universal authorities. An adult might also suppose that another adult already knew or was able to find out just about anything worth knowing at all, and treat him as a universal authority. If our authority is not supposed to know everything already but simply to be able to find out what others know, then one might indeed have some reason to think him worth taking seriously on all subjects. If he does not already know about some matter, he can consult someone who does or some book that will tell him. And are not libraries supposed to be storehouses of knowledge, in which one might be able to find answers to any question that can be answered at all?

Bases of Authority

People come to have influence over our thoughts in a variety of ways. However they acquire such influence, as long as we think it right that they should have it, we will be prepared to defend and justify their influence. We will have answers to the questions," Why do you listen to him?" and "Why do you let him influence you so?" The answer "because he knows so much" will not be enough, for the question then becomes, "What makes you think so?" Our task now is to explore the available answers to that question: the kinds of answers conventionally recognized as appropriate. The situation is not one in which we, as ourselves knowledgeable in a certain sphere, have examined others to see how much they know about this sphere. Whatever our reasons for thinking the others deserving of cognitive authority, it is not that we have conducted a direct test of their knowledge. Rather, we have to cite indirect tests or indexes of credibility. The situation is one in which we may be faced with a number of different people all claiming to be knowledgeable but all having different things to say on the same subject. Given that we ourselves are not knowledgeable on the subject, how can we choose among them, or how can we defend our choice once made?

There are quite conventional ways of answering these questions, as there should be, for the questions come up repeatedly in ordinary life. A standard answer to the question, "What qualifies him to speak on the subject?" is that it is his business; he makes his living dealing with that subject. The old practical rule is that *cuique in arte suā credendum*, each one is to be trusted in matters of his own metier; occupational specialization provides a basis for recognition of cognitive authority. An equally familiar answer is that he has studied the subject systematically and deeply and has earned advanced degrees in the subject. To the old occupational rule we have added the new rule of formal education, with its corollary, the credential or degree, as evidence of successful completion of programs of formal study. These two bases for cognitive authority are recognized in our courts of law. Expert witnesses must be shown to be qualified as experts by "knowledge, skill, experience, training, or education." Barring a direct test of knowledge or skill, which we

cannot administer when we are not ourselves already knowledgeable, evidence of training or education or of practical experience, especially in an occupational role, provides support
for claims to expert status.[9]

One can be an expert without being a great expert. Experience
and education are taken as evidence of a basic but not outstanding competence. As a practical matter, we take reputation among
others who are supposed to be experts in the same line of work
or study as indication of outstanding competence. A "leading
expert in the field" is recognized as such simply by discovering
that other practitioners in the same field think highly of him.
Dependence on peer opinion means that we have no way of
identifying those neglected or unrecognized geniuses who are
unduly or improperly ignored or denigrated by their peers, but
there is nothing we can do about that if we lack independent
tests of competence.

The reputation rule for identifying great experts is not a simple
one, for a reputation may be high in one group of supposed
peers and low in another, and it is not always reputation among
peers that is taken to count. One might have a great reputation
among those outside the peer group and a lesser one inside.
The outsiders' opinions may outweigh the insiders'. The reputation rule will work unambiguously in many cases but in others
will give different results depending on how one chooses the
appropriate group, the reference group, whose collective opinion is taken as an index of competence.

There is another reputation rule, of the greatest practical importance. If those of whom I myself think well think well of
person A, then I will incline to think well of A and think myself
justified in doing so. If those whose word counts heavily with
me say that A's word counts heavily with them, I will be inclined
to recognize A as having cognitive authority. Those already established as my cognitive authorities can transfer authority to
another. I believe him because I believe them, and they say that
he can be believed. As reputation among peers unknown to me
can be taken to provide an indirect test of competence, so can
reputation among the special group of people who are already
trusted as knowledgeable. This is simply the omnipresent phenomenon of personal recommendation. As the old boy network,

it has a bad name, but as the principle that one can trust those who are trusted by those one trusts, it is a central and ineradicable feature of social life. We cling to this rule to find our way through the confusion of life.

We should make a special place for common consent as a basis of cognitive authority. If everyone recognizes A as an authority in a sphere, I am likely to do so as well and think myself justified in doing so. This amounts to a generalization of the two other reputation rules. First, if my own authorities and everybody else say that A is wise, that is a good reason for me to think him wise. Second, if A's colleagues all think him wise and everyone else does too, that is good reason for me to think him wise. Reputation is not proof of wisdom, knowledge, or competence, but we take it as a reasonable basis for preferring to listen to one person rather than another.

Any kind of successful accomplishment may be taken as an index of special competence. Quite apart from the reputation a person has among various groups, we may think ourselves able to evaluate the person's performances and may use the evaluation as a basis for recognition of cognitive authority. The general principle is this: If a person can achieve striking results of whatever kind in some area of life, then he must have whatever knowledge it takes to do this and is deserving of being recognized as a cognitive authority in that area. Of course, this performance rule is applicable only when the performance to be judged is something other than the creation or articulation of theory or doctrine, for that is just the sort of performance we will be unable to evaluate for ourselves. To make predictions that we ourselves can verify, to produce startling effects—miracles, prodigies—that we ourselves can witness, is to give us an indirect ground for supposing that the performer has some special competence. The doctor who cures patients (especially those given up for lost by other doctors), the general who wins campaigns (especially if quickly, or at little cost in life, or against great odds), the entrepreneur who founds great business empires, may be held by virtue of these performances to have what it takes to do these things and to be eligible as cognitive authorities. Those who attain great power or wealth by their own efforts may qualify under the same principle. Just what will be the sphere within which authority is recognized is another matter.

When available, this performance rule is a powerful one for justifying recognition of cognitive authority. Since reputations are based on performance (not exclusively, but in large part), this rule underlies the reputation rule. We use the reputation rule in cases where we cannot ourselves evaluate the performances on which reputation is based. But the performance test is often unavailable and often inconclusive. The scholar makes no predictions that others might confirm or disconfirm, cures no ills, performs no miracles, but simply tries to discover what is true and what is false in his area of inquiry. There is no external test of successful accomplishment for the outsider to apply. Where there is an external performance, success is often ambiguous. It is not clear that the patient has benefitted from the doctor's treatment; we cannot tell whether the economist's advice has improved matters, for it is not clear that matters are improved. Or improvement is not clearly due to treatment: the patient feels better but we cannot tell if it was the doctor's treatment that was responsible. Or we are sure that treatment produced results but wonder if treatment really was based on a special fund of knowledge at all, rather than on luck or on an ability the doctor has but does not really understand. Or results of the performance will show up only in the long run, and we cannot now tell whether it was a success. Or results of performance are closely guarded secrets or discoverable only by an effort that is too great to be practical. There are so many cases in which the performance rule is not available at all or is inconclusive that it cannot serve us as the principal basis for justifying cognitive authority.

We have been considering indirect ways of justifying the recognition of cognitive authority, but there is one crucial direct way that cannot be ignored. Authority can be justified simply on the ground that one finds the views of an individual intrinsically plausible, convincing, or persuasive. If a source repeatedly tells me things that I find illuminating and that ring true, I may come to expect more of the same from him, to count on him, refer others to him, quote him to others. He will have acquired cognitive authority over me. As can any other authority, he can lose it too by failing to continue to say things that impress me in the same way. And one who on other grounds—of experience, training, reputation, ostensible performance—might claim cognitive authority will not acquire it if what he tells me fails the test of intrinsic plausibility. I simply cannot take seriously views that are so blatantly implausible.

The test of intrinsic plausibility is not available for many spheres of interest. What a specialist has to say may be so remote from my own experience and so distant from any of my established beliefs about the world that it is neither plausible nor implausible. The closer the specialist comes to talking of matters on which I already have a stock of beliefs and convictions, the more likely it is that the plausibility test will be available and will discriminate among opposing views. Our prior beliefs set limits to what we can accept as new beliefs and guide us in the acceptance of others as cognitive authorities. What we cannot believe and what we find it easy to believe among the new things we are told depend heavily on what we already believed. The plausibility test, where it applies, overrides all other reasons for accepting or rejecting authority—or all but one.

Finally, authority can be acquired and defended on the basis simply of personal trust, belief in a person. Particularly striking cases are those of what Max Weber called charismatic authority.[10] The prophet, the hero, the saint may attract a complete personal devotion that carries with it a readiness to let the individual define his own sphere of cognitive authority. In less extreme cases, we may be so impressed by a person, so attracted or mesmerized by him that we are prepared to believe whatever he says. We need no external tests of extraordinary performance (though these may be available), no evidence of reputation (though this may in fact influence us), no credentials or degrees; the direct impression of the individual personality may be enough. Even the ordinarily final test of intrinsic plausibility may be overridden. We may be converted to new views. In conversion we undergo the sort of internal revolution that makes nonsense into sense, the implausible plausible, the odious attractive, and all—at least apparently—in the twinkling of an eye. Not only religious and political figures acquire cognitive authority in this way; the followers of a founder of a scientific school may become followers in the same way and for the same

reason that the followers of a religious prophet become followers, though they will probably be adept at finding other reasons
for adhering to the doctrine of the great teacher.

Any of these various bases of authority might be cited in
defense of one's reliance on the word of another; clearly any of
them might be challenged. They are all recognizably legitimate
or appropriate to mention. We all at one time or another appeal
to experience, training, publicly appraisable accomplishment,
reputation among peers, reputation among our other cognitive
authorities, intrinsic plausibility, and think it proper to do so.
The final appeal, to one's trust in an individual, may seem the
least rational or objective but may also be recognized as the most
compelling and unchallengeable—unchallengeable not because
trust proves anything but because it is uncontrollable, irresistible, and so outside the realm of deliberate choice. But they are
all inconclusive, mere signs or indexes of legitimacy of cognitive
authority. None of them is sufficient to establish authority beyond any challenge and none of them is sufficient to determine
either the sphere of authority or the degree of authority even
when recognition of some authority in some sphere is not challenged. It is worth dwelling on the degree to which justifications
of cognitive authority can be porous. We will concentrate on the
difficult relationship between expertise and authority.

Expertise and Authority

We generally use the terms *expert* and *authority* interchange-
ably; the authorities on a subject are the experts in that subject,
and vice versa. This is natural enough since we take expertise
to mean the possession of some special body of knowledge and
authority to rest on the possession of knowledge. But it is a good
idea to put some space between the ideas of expertise and authority and to be cautious about the connection between them.
Although the expert may have some special body of knowledge,
it may not be knowledge about the world and may not warrant
recognition of authority. We can comfortably ignore the difference between expertise and authority only by assuming that the
experts are not only experts about something but that what they
are expert about is some field of real knowledge of the world.
If we no longer recognize authorities in astrology, it is because

we no longer believe that astrologists possess a special body of knowledge about the world; but we can still recognize a difference between inexpert and expert astrologists. The experts may not know anything special about the world, but they do know something that novice astrologists do not. Astrology has bodies of doctrine, and some people are (or were, especially when astrology was an academic subject) better than others at the exposition, development, and application of doctrine.[11] The question is whether one should believe even a very expert astrologist, whether expertise warrants cognitive authority. For most of us (or most sensible people—there are huge numbers of people for whom astrology is still a serious subject with serious authorities), the answer is that it does not.[12] There is expertise without authority. Neither long practical experience nor systematic study leading to higher degrees in astrology will support a claim of cognitive authority, though they will support a claim of expertise.

The question arises whether there are not other examples of expertise without knowledge, expertise that does not justify authority. Not only are there brands of expertise no longer regarded as corresponding to any real knowledge; there are numerous instances of competing brands of expertise all claiming authority in the same sphere, and the question arises which brand, if any of them, is the right brand of expertise to warrant cognitive authority. It is not just that there are different people claiming expertise, among whom we may want or have to choose, but that there are different kinds of expertise among which we may have to choose. So we have a double problem: first, to choose among competing brands of expertise, and then to select a particular expert representing the chosen brand.

In practice the two problems may not be seen as two: the jury members, faced with conflicting expert testimony from representatives of two conflicting brands of psychotherapy, may telescope the two questions into a single one, of what weight (the term used in discussions of the law of evidence) to give the testimony of each. But the distinction remains. Different theologies compete to be recognized as authoritative in matters of the supernatural. Different brands of economic analysis compete to be recognized as authoritative in matters of diagnosis and therapy for economic ills. Different psychotherapies compete in the sphere of questions of mental health and illness. We can recognize a person's expertise in a particular line of doctrine and inquiry while still wondering whether he should be taken seriously on substantive questions within the sphere he claims to occupy. And we may decide that the leading experts in their field really have nothing to tell us that is worth knowing. If evidence of experience or training is evidence of expertise, it is a long jump from expertise to authority. We may often make the jump without thinking; it may take the emergence of a public controversy over the rival claims of competing brands of expertise to make us wonder whether we should make it.

Even when recognized expertise is taken to warrant cognitive authority, the sphere of authority remains to be settled. The law is careful to insist that one's claim to expert standing is valid only within one's specific field of expertise. The doctor is not asked to testify as an expert witness on matters outside the range of his medical specialty. Outside the court of law, things are not so clear. There the sphere of cognitive authority is often negotiated by the authority and his audience to extend far beyond what the specialist thinks is the core area of his expertise, or to be restricted to a small part of the area over which he is willing to claim authority. We may be inclined to think that there is an objective or at least universally recognized rule governing the scope for which expertise justifies cognitive authority: a rule of specialization, that authority must not be claimed or recognized on any question outside the area within which one can claim expertise. But the rule is not generally accepted and is not very solid in any case. Authority is recognized far beyond the limits of specialization.

We recognize the existence of generalists, people to whom we can turn for advice on a wide range of questions, much wider than that within which they would claim to be specialists. It is to the generalist, for example, that one has to turn for advice on how to treat competing specialties; it is no good asking the specialists. The people whose views on social, political, and ethical matters we value most are unlikely to be people who speak strictly as specialists and only on questions falling within the scope of a specialty. But there are interesting individual and national differences of attitude to different kinds of generalists. One of the striking differences between France and the United States, to take a glaring instance, concerns public expectations of eminent literary artists and intellectuals. As one perceptive European observer notes, "No American would think of going to a novelist or dramatist for advice on civic or social questions, for such questions fall within the competence of 'experts' only". In France, by contrast, the great writers are *maîtres à penser*, teachers of thinking, and recognized as sources of serious opinion and advice on a wide range of social and political topics.[13] A French commentator provides an American-like version of the same situation: in France "writers with no authority whatsoever can obtain large audiences even when they treat of subjects about which they quite openly boast of knowing nothing—a phenomenon which is inconceivable in the United States."[14] But Americans, or many of them, would think it appropriate to turn to a successful businessman for advice on civic or social questions, or to a successful general for advice on political or administrative questions. Successful accomplishment is taken to justify recognition of cognitive authority in areas far from the immediate field of accomplishment, though people (and nations) differ as to what sorts of accomplishment justify what sort of sphere of cognitive authority.

But the rule of specialization is at best elastic. An area of specialization can be variously described and interpreted. Taking the narrowest view, one might suppose a person qualified as an expert only with regard to questions that one had already answered oneself by original, independent research; a person would be an expert only on his own original work. At the other extreme, one might be supposed to be qualified as an expert with regard to questions that one's own work had put one in a position to illumine, if not to settle, questions to which the point of view and the training and experience acquired as a specialist were relevant and helpful. In that case, the businessman, the general, the artist might all plausibly claim that their work in their home fields did indeed qualify them as experts in relation to questions remote from home. After all, they have to deal with human nature, social organization, plans, and implementation of plans, and their experience allows them to make sense of a wide variety of human situations. Such a claim of transferable competence or wide-ranging expertise may be ridiculous in any particular case, but the general claim is not obviously nonsensical. So whether by ignoring or bending the rule of specialization, we recognize cognitive authority far beyond what a narrow reading of the rule would warrant.

By now it will be apparent that as appeal to expertise does not settle the question of spheres of authority, neither does it settle the question of degrees of authority. How much weight it is appropriate to give to the words of an expert specialist or a generalist within the appropriate sphere of authority is a practical question to which there appear to be no ready conventional answers. The members of the jury are left to decide for themselves what weight should be given to expert testimony, with no instruction on how this can or should be done. The problem is serious, but any attempt to clarify it immediately takes us into deep and dark waters of ignorance. Let us cautiously try for some small advance in understanding.

Do We Believe Our Authorities?

We have to talk about memory. Much of what we have heard or read remains in memory with a label attached, recording where and when we heard or read it. Of course we immediately forget much of what we hear or read. Of the part that we remember, we tend to recall the source as well as some version of the content. After a while we may forget the source while retaining the content, though after we forget who told us or where we read it, we will still remember that someone told us or that we read it somewhere. It is as if the source label was defaced or faded beyond reading. Something heard from several sources may be remembered simply as something "they" say, the "they" being no longer individually identifiable after a while. Information acquired a long time ago may be recalled as "what they taught us in school," "what the books tell you to do in a case like this," and "what people used to say about him."

Do we believe what we are told? Certainly not everything. I recall hearing Smith say that Brown was vindictive, but I do not believe it. I have heard people say that Jones is ambitious, and

I do think that is right. I am told that Green is going to run for president, but I have no idea whether that is so. Clearly we need not have an opinion on the truth or falsity of something we have heard, even when we recollect hearing it and remember where and when we heard it.

What about things we have heard from those who are cognitive authorities for us? What happens to those bits of information or advice? One might have supposed that cognitive authorities served as automatic sources of new beliefs—that if one whom I recognize as an authority tells me that so and so, I immediately acquire the belief that so and so, which I would then explain or defend as something I now know because I heard it from my authority on the subject. This can indeed happen, and if it always happens with that authority, he is an absolute authority for me. But we have already argued that this is a limiting rather than the usual case. The most obvious and, for many people, most attractive alternative view is that the authority's word changes the probability that I assign to the statement or proposition that the authority asserts.[15] If my authority tells me that bacon causes cancer, the degree of probability that I assign to the proposition that bacon causes cancer goes up and the greater his authority, the more it goes up. Since my beliefs are not discrete, independent items, when the probability of one such proposition changes, the probabilities of other logically related propositions will have to change too if I am to maintain consistency. Thus one word from the authority sets in motion (or should do so) a whole train of mental readjustments.

This view of the mind makes it too much of a logic machine. It may accurately describe what happens sometimes, or perhaps always in some people, but for some of us at least it is an unlikely story. It seems more plausible to suppose that much of what we hear from our authorities gets filed away in the "hearsay collection" in our memory, with the source duly noted on the label.[16] We neither believe nor disbelieve it; we simply file it away for future reference. Until one has to use it in some way, it can remain simply a recollected piece of hearsay. When the time comes, if ever, to take an action, make a plan, or simply answer a question to which such a remembered item is relevant, we can recall it and evaluate it. Then, but not until then, we face the question of what weight to give to the source. But even then we need not go about assigning probabilities to the recollected item. We may simply want to decide whether to act on the assumption that what the authority said is true, to act as if we believe it. (There are those who would say that to act as if you believe it is to believe it, but this is certainly not so. We frequently have to act as if things were so that we know are not.) If the authority's word carries much weight, is not opposed by contrary authorities, and is consistent with what else we believe and think relevant, then we will take the authority's word for it, which is not the same thing as coming to believe him. In more complicated cases, we may have to engage in a quasi-judicial process, balancing what this authority says against what that authority says, adding what we ourselves believe on the basis of our own experience and reflection. And what happens in that process is something we ourselves do not understand. An interior monologue reporting on the process might run like this: "I find myself much impressed by what A said, and of course he's had a great deal of experience in matters like this. On the other hand, what B says is not implausible, it certainly might be true, and he does have impressive qualifications. But when it comes down to a decision, I find that I am more drawn to A's side than to B's." We are not deciding how much weight to give; we are finding how much we do give. The only control we have over the process is control over the attention we give to the different parties, the time we take to listen, the time we devote to reflecting on what we are told. The reason juries are given no instructions on how to assign weights to testimony is that assigning weight is not something we can do; it is something that happens to us. It can happen differently under different circumstances, and our only practical wisdom is that it happens best in circumstances under which we give careful attention to the alternative positions. The question of how much weight should be given to the words of an authority is to be settled only by giving a fair hearing to him and seeing what happens to one's thoughts. It is misleading to say that "it is for the trier of fact to decide what weight should be accorded the testimony of expert witnesses." There is no decision, but a happening of another sort.[17]

Results

Looking around the social world, we find an astonishing variety of bizarre belief systems—bizarre to us, not to their holders. Fantastic religious beliefs, repulsive moral beliefs, crazy economic theories, bigoted political creeds . . . the list goes on until we tire of adding to it. It is true that we know very little about the beliefs of most other people. That a person is, for example, a practicng Mormon or Catholic or Christian Scientist tells us virtually nothing about their religious beliefs. The ordinary adherents of a religion cannot be expected to know much about the details of the official orthodox creed to which they nominally subscribe, and we scarcely have the time, even if we had the inclination and the cooperation of the others, to make exhaustive inquiries into the content of their beliefs.

Reliance on published statements by articulate defenders of the myriad positions on religious, moral, economic, social, and other matters is a poor way of finding out what ordinary people think. Public opinion polls are superficial and unreliable tools for exploring ordinary beliefs. Our own personal samples, of the few people we know intimately enough to have acquired some detailed knowledge of their beliefs, are inevitably biased by the accident of our social location. The people we know best tend to be much like ourselves, and generalization from what our friends think to what people in general think is sure to go wrong. Still, a careful look around provides plenty of evidence that the world is full of people who are not only ignorant of things we think they should know about but also full of mistaken, often fantastic notions as well. And prominent are mistaken recognitions of cognitive authority. People are followers of false prophets, deluded theorists, leaders of pseudo-scientific cults, leaders with undeserved reputations for wisdom. How does all this happen? Why do people not share our own sensible beliefs? Why can they not recognize the truth when they see it? Does the fault lie in the way in which they acquire their cognitive authorities? Are they doing something wrong, or are they just unlucky? Whatever the cause, the results are unfortunate.

We are not yet in a position to say how it is that people come to have influence over our thoughts, but we now have the in-

ventory, or most of the inventory, of considerations that are
thought to be relevant in justifying a recognition of authority.
Perhaps there is something systematically wrong with our notions of what is relevant. Let us look back to the rule of reputation, either among peers or among one's own cognitive
authorities. Either can lead to terrible results. This general is
much admired by fellow generals, so we take his advice on how
to conduct the campaign, and look what happens: terrible
slaughter and final defeat. My friends tell me that that fellow
Hitler is the man to listen to, so I do. But can we imagine giving
up the reputation rules? Certainly we cannot simply invert the
rules and always give credence to those of no reputation, or a
low reputation, or despised by those we trust. Or consider the
rule of plausibility, the use of one's own prior knowledge as a
test of the intrinsic plausibility of cognitive claims. I am not going
to pay any attention to some new messiah's claims to be in direct
communication with the deity; without examination, I dismiss
the claim out of hand. Similarly, I reject out of hand the idea of
flying machines; they cannot possibly work, and so I need pay
no attention to those Wright brothers. A chapter entitled "The
Stupidity of Doubt" in a book on human stupidity is full of
examples of learned men dismissing important discoveries on
the ground that they could not be real, based on what one
already knew.[18] These are bad results; but can we imagine not
bringing our preconceived ideas to test the plausibility of new
things we hear? This is one of the chief things minds are for: to
tell us what is likely and what not. It is not possible for us to
turn off our judgment without turning off our minds. Our prior
beliefs definitely prejudice us against many new beliefs, and
although we can try to give a fair hearing to novel claims, we
cannot avoid the influence of prior belief. But why should we
want to? Do we really think we would do better with empty
heads?

The different bases for justifying cognitive authority are all
accident-prone, highly fallible guides, but we cannot do without
them. Perhaps, however, the trouble comes in some systematic
misapplication of them. Let us think about familiar defects. Common sense and ordinary experience lead us to recognize the
polar defects of credulity and excessive skepticism. Some people

regularly, and most people occasionally, are too easily persuaded of the superior knowledge of others. They tend to believe whatever they read or hear, suffer from primitive credulity, are overly impressed by credentials, overgeneralize from accomplishment in one field to competence in widely dissimilar fields, are too impressed by reputation—in general, too easily persuaded.[19] At the other end are the dour skeptics who are full of distrust for all reputations, all credentials, all so-called accomplishments, full of mulish resistance to persuasion, resentment of all authority, hostility to elitist claims to superior knowledge, sullen insistence that their opinion is as good as anyone's. Both of these defects—there is no question, is there, that they are defects?—are familiar; it is not so clear that they are remediable. Nor is it clear that there is any general way of calibrating degrees of credulity and spotting a point or region that is just right. Nor, finally, is it clear that these defects are the ones responsible for the odd patterns of belief we find around us. It is a wickedly effective propaganda weapon to accuse those who hold views we think wicked or stupid of credulity, of too easy acceptance of authority. But such charges can be made with equal ease on all sides; they are symmetrical. Are liberals more or less credulous than conservatives? Is belief in Catholic dogma, or atheism, the result of excessive credulity or of pigheadedness in rejecting other views? It seems likely that no side in any dispute has a monopoly on adherents suffering from the polar faults. Those faults are not systematically sources of bias toward error. One's credulity can lead one to the truth, and one's obstinacy can prevent one from falling into error. With equal likelihood, one's obstinacy can keep one from the truth and one's credulity lead one into error.

If we are to understand the diversity of belief, it will have to be in terms not of bases for justification or of patterns of their application but in historical terms—the historical circumstances leading to an initial outfitting with a stock of beliefs, and the subsequent history of encounters with people and ideas.

Notes

1. Bochenski and De George speak of epistemic authority rather than of cognitive authority: J. M. Bochenski, "On Authority," *Memorias*

del XIII Congreso Internacional de Filosofía, México, D.F., 1963, Comunicaciones Libres, Sección I & II (México, D.F.: Universidad Nacional Autónoma de México, 1964), 5: 45-46; Richard T. De George, "The Nature and Function of Epistemic Authority," in *Authority: A Philosophical Analysis*, ed. R. Baine Harris (University: University of Alabama Press, 1976), pp. 76-93. On the subject of this chapter, see the early work of George Cornewall Lewis, *An Essay on the Influence of Authority in Matters of Opinion*, 2d ed. (London: Longmans, Green, 1875), full of historical references. For bibliography of philosophical works on authority, see the bibliography by De George in *Authority*, pp. 141-70. There is strangely little of direct relevance. Epistemologists have had little to say about the evidence of testimony, and Price claims there are not even any standard views on the subject. H. H. Price, *Belief* (London: Allen & Unwin, 1969), p. 111.

2. The analyses given by Bochenski and De George are similar to this one, except that they would say that the authority is one whose word increases the probability that I would attach to some proposition. But De George often talks of weight rather than probability.

3. This makes all authority legitimate, which seems to me proper; illegitimate authority is no authority. See Charles W. Hendel, "An Exploration of the Nature of Authority," in *Authority*, ed. Carl J. Friedrich, Nomos 1 (Cambridge: Harvard University Press, 1958), pp. 3-27, esp. p. 14.

4. See Herbert A. Simon, "Authority," in *Research in Industrial Human Relations, A Critical Appraisal*, Industrial Relations Research Association Pubn. no. 17 (New York: Harper, 1957), pp. 103-15 and his *Administrative Behavior*, 2d ed. (New York: Free Press, 1965), Ch. 7.

5. Daryl J. Bem, *Beliefs, Attitudes, and Human Affairs* (Belmont, Calif.: Brooks/Cole, 1970), pp. 71-75.

6. Cf. Wigmore on evidence: "It is misleading to think of some witnesses as experts and others as nonexperts. Every witness whosoever is and must be, by hypothesis, fitted or 'expert' in the matter about which he is allowed to give his supposed knowledge." John Henry Wigmore, *A Treatise on the Anglo-American System of Evidence in Trials at Common Law*, 3d ed. (Boston: Little, Brown, 1940), 10: 634.

7. Ibid., pp. 633-35.

8. On "belief in," see Price, *Belief*, pp. 426-54.

9. *Moore's Federal Practice*, 2d ed., vol. 11: *Federal Rules of Evidence*, by James Wm. Moore and Helen I. Bendix (New York: Bender, 1976), Rule 702, "Testimony by Experts." A person may become qualified as an expert by practical experience and home study; professional education is not a prerequisite.

10. Max Weber, *The Theory of Social and Economic Organization*, ed. Talcott Parsons (New York: Free Press, 1964), pp. 358-63.

11. On "academic astrology," see Carolly Erickson, *The Medieval Vision* (New York: Oxford University Press, 1976), pp. 22-27.

12. On belief in astrology, see Gustav Jahoda, *The Psychology of Superstition* (London: Allen Lane, 1969); Mircea Eliade, *Occultism, Witchcraft and Cultural Fashions* (Chicago: University of Chicago Press, 1976), Ch. 4; Claude Fischler, "Astrology and French Society: The Dialectic of Archaism and Modernity," in *On the Margin of the Visible*, ed. Edward A. Tiryakian (New York: Wiley, 1974), pp. 281-93.

13. Jean Améry, *Preface to the Future: Culture in a Consumer Society* (New York: Ungar, 1964), p. 88. Cf. Régis Debray, *Teachers, Writers, Celebrities: The Intellectuals of Modern France* (London: Verso, 1981), and Jane Kramer, "A Reporter in Europe: Paris," *New Yorker*, 30 June 1980, pp. 42-54.

14. Raymond Aron, quoted in Harold Rosenberg, *Discovering the Present* (Chicago: University of Chicago Press, 1973), p. 168.

15. See note 2 above.

16. I do not mean to imply any particular model of the physical organization of memory or to suggest that memories are discrete items, like different sentences in a collection of sentences. On the question of whether we believe what our authorities tell us, compare Ferdinand C. S. Schiller, *Problems of Belief* (London: Hodder & Stoughton, 1924), p. 56: "Thus beliefs accepted on authority, and not acquired by the believer's own efforts, are apt never to grow into anything more substantial than half-beliefs."

17. The quotation is from *Moore's Federal Practice*, Rule 702.30(2), p. VII-35.

18. Paul Tabori, *The Natural Science of Stupidity* (Philadelphia: Chilton, 1959), Ch. 7.

19. The phrase *primitive credulity* comes from Alexander Bain, the nineteenth-century British philosopher.

3 THE KNOWLEDGE INDUSTRY: QUALITY AND FASHION

Industry Analysis

It has become common to speak of a knowledge industry, in which people work at the systematic production of new knowledge.[1] Let us accept the idea of an industry devoted to the production of knowledge but only in the sense of a group of people systematically trying to produce knowledge. We should not start with the assumption that the attempt is invariably or generally successful. Perhaps the industry produces not knowledge but opinion; perhaps, that is, it does not manage to settle the questions it addresses but manages only to produce a variety of answers, leaving the questions open. And perhaps it produces both. This is what we would like to find out: what the knowledge industry produces.

Let us assume that the industry includes all those whose work is to try to find out new things about the world and also to analyze, synthesize, interpret, improve, and evaluate the claims of others. *Research* is the term most often used for what the workers in this industry do, but *inquiry* is better, since it can be understood to include those activities of synthesis, interpretation, and evaluation that would not usually be considered research. The industry includes those working in the formal, natural, and social sciences and in the humanities. Attempts to improve technology, to find new and better ways of doing and making things, are certainly attempts to add to the available stock of knowledge, and the improvers of technology are workers in the knowledge industry; but we will not consider their branch of the industry. What they try to produce are new devices and new procedures; what those in the part of the industry we are concerned with try to produce are new views. The improvers of technology try to produce new know-how, the others try to produce new knowledge-that, or propositional knowledge.

We will also ignore the many kinds of inquiry that are not respectable or socially established. Inquiries into astrology, telepathy, clairvoyance, telekinesis, and extrasensory perception can be considered as part of an "underground" knowledge industry, which we can ignore for the present, though remembering that what is not respectable today may become respectable tomorrow.

We would like to know if knowledge is indeed produced in the knowledge industry and if it is knowledge worth having. We will begin our attempt to answer these questions in this chapter, and conclude it in the next. Here we will treat them as questions of quality: what can we say about the way in which one determines the quality of the products of the industry? In order to approach this subject, it is necessary first to consider the organization of the industry, for it is crucial for understanding evaluation of work in the industry.

The basic unit of industry analysis is usually the enterprise or establishment: business firms, for example, or individual factory or business premises. For the analysis of this industry, it seems better to consider the basic producing unit to be the individual worker or team of workers. In some branches of our industry, the individual producer customarily works alone; in other branches, producers work in teams of from two to hundreds of people.[2] A single academic working with the part-time help of a student constitutes a team, usually a short-lived one. Teams are unstable. The team assembled to do a particular piece of work disbands on its completion, and a somewhat different team assembles for the next piece of work. Unlike other industries where the same firm or enterprise or establishment may continue for years to produce the same product with a slowly changing work force, in this industry each piece of work differs from the others. But any producer still turns out only a limited number of types of product.

Workers and work done can be classified into different specialties, consisting of producers who are producing the same sort of product, or at any rate trying to do so. The definition of a specialty is of great difficulty; the notion of a specialty is loose and elastic.[3] We may say that workers in the same specialty are those who recognize each other as engaged in the same kind of work and who might at any time find themselves in direct competition (whether or not they ever actually do).[4] They are those who recognize roughly the same range of problems as being within their scope of competence and interest. A specialty may be narrow or wide, depending on the range of problems among which the members are able to move freely.

Specialties are located in larger areas of inquiry, which we can call fields, and may themselves be divisible into subspecialties. The number of producers in a specialty may be large or small, independently of whether the specialty is wide or narrow. Ordinarily specialties are small in membership. In the natural sciences, most scientists are likely to know personally all those doing similar work.[5] Specialties may have only one member; a person may do work of a sort that no one else in the world is doing, studying phenomena that no one else studies (as in mathematics or systematics), or studying what others also study but in a way different from all others' ways.[6] Whether a person is a solo specialist or an idiosyncratic member of a populous specialty will often be hard or impossible to decide. An individual may belong to several specialties at the same time; he may not belong to any but be a generalist working occasionally at problems usually falling within the scope of particular specialties but not considering himself or being considered by others as a member of any specialty group. Membership in a specialty is not well defined and not stable; specialties themselves are unstable and ill-defined groups.

The work done in the industry can be approximately divided into distinct pieces or jobs, though the division is rough and arbitrary. For our purposes it will be convenient to divide these pieces or jobs—we will call them projects—into two groups: self-selected projects and other-selected projects. Scholars working alone in a university ordinarily select their own projects. Scientists or technicians working in an industrial laboratory may have their projects selected for them by others or be told to work with this group on a project already defined by others. An independent research organization that contracts with a government agency to perform a piece of research defined by the agency does indeed freely choose to bid for the contract and so might be said to work on a self-selected project. We will describe their work as other-selected, however, since the reason the work is accomplished is that the agency, not the research organization itself, decided that it should be done and decided how it should be done. On the other hand, a scientist's research may be entirely supported by federal funds given in the form of a grant. The funding agency does freely decide to support the work, does then choose it for support, but we will describe the work as self-selected since the scientist originates the proposal. The point is that other-selected work is work done to meet a specific external demand; someone else has a specific interest in the work. The kind of work to be done and the acceptability of the work actually done is determined by those who set the problem and decide the amount of support to be allowed to its solution. What is done, and whether it is well enough done, are decided outside the specialty group.

The public opinion research organization that conducts a survey for a business firm is responsible primarily to the firm; whether it tells the firm what it wants to know is the criterion of acceptability. On the other hand, the scientist or scholar working on self-selected projects works under quite different conditions. He may have to persuade an outside agency that his project is worth support and may revise the project until he can persuade someone to support it.[7] But the supporting agency may have no specific need for this particular piece of work; it may support it simply because it seems worthwhile. And whether it turns out to be worthwhile is judged not by the agency but by the specialist's peers within the specialty. So universities support the research of their faculty members by allowing them time for research; the university has no specific need for the research done by its faculty members, and the worth of particular pieces of research is judged primarily by the worker's peers.

The ostensible aim of self-selected work in the knowledge industry may be the production of knowledge, but its first and most obvious product is paper.[8] One working on an other-selected project may be allowed to publish one's results, but publication is not the primary goal, and of course much industrial and governmentally sponsored research is meant to be kept secret. Self-selected work aims at publication. We can divide the knowledge industry into public and private sectors, not on the usual basis (privately owned, profit-making enterprises versus publicly owned, nonprofit enterprises) but by whether work is or is not made public by being published. And having made the distinction, we can exclude the private sector from further consideration.

It is the public sector of the knowledge industry that concerns us. This includes the results of such other-selected projects as do get made public but excludes a large body of work that may otherwise be indistinguishable in character and quality from work made public. Many discussions of science and scholarship essentially assume that all research is self-selected, a serious error, particularly for understanding scientific production. But we are interested in evaluation, and specifically in the evaluation of work not done on demand to meet specific requirements of someone outside the specialty, and so can ignore private-sector work. This means we are ignoring a good deal of applied science. Presumably most pure research is self-selected work in the public sector.

Work in the public sector of the industry aims at making additions to the body of public knowledge, knowledge in principle open and available to everyone. Individual workers not only try to make such additions but also to be recognized as having done so. Workers in this industry do not seek anonymity. They seek reputation, which depends on how much of a contribution one is thought to have made to the increase of public knowledge. Reputation is not (or not exclusively) sought for its own sake but for the recognition of cognitive authority that will be based on it. One can view the public sector of the knowledge industry as a collection of arenas of struggle for authority. Each actor in the arena tries to force others to recognize him as having the highest possible degree of cognitive authority within the sphere of the struggle.[9] The chief way of doing this is by making contributions that the others working in the same area find themselves, however reluctantly, compelled to recognize as interesting and important; and the contributions must be public—that is, published. Reputation does not vary directly with quantity of publication; quality as perceived by one's fellow specialists does count.[10] But without publications, one can extract little recognition of cognitive authority except from the few with whom one has close personal contact. Publication is essential for new entrants into a specialty. Only by publication does one establish oneself as an independent member of the group in full standing, acquire job security and job mobility, and begin to acquire a reputation. The slogan "publish or perish" describes the situation exactly. In a university, people "are hired, to put it baldly, on the basis of how good they will look to others. . . . There is very little point in trying to determine how good the man *really* is. What is important is what others in the discipline think of him, since that is, in large part, how good he *is*."[11] And what others think will depend on their perceptions of the quality and quantity of publication.

Each piece of work produced in a specialty will exemplify a certain research style. The notion of style applies to inquiry quite as well as it does to works of art or indeed to any other complex human activity or production. Description of a research style might include any characteristic feature of a person's or a group's way of working: kinds of problems selected, kinds of concepts and theories and experimental techniques and methods of analysis employed, kinds of explanations attempted, kinds of evidence deployed, and so on. Analysis of research style includes, if it is not identical with, analysis of patterns of choice: choice of what to study and of ways of studying it and of presenting the results of one's work.[12] Explicit analyses of research style are not abundant but also not rare. For example, a psychologist contrasting two styles of attitude research writes: "The Hovland style is convergent, while the Festinger [style] is divergent . . . .The Hovlanders take much more care in measuring the dependent variable and the intervening processes . . .they are rather cavalier about independent variable manipulation . . . .The Festingerians, on the other hand, utilize extremely clever and elaborate manipulations of the independent variable, but are rather offhand in measuring the effect on the dependent variable."[13]

Any sort of intellectual work is susceptible to analogous stylistic analysis. Careful analysis of an individual producer's style would always, one supposes, reveal unique features. Each worker has his own style, different to some degree from those of his peers. But co-workers in a specialty are likely to work in similar styles and indeed probably would recognize others as co-workers only if their styles of work were sufficiently similar. As in the world of art, a common style provides "a common ground against which innovations and the individuality of particular works may be measured."[14] As in the world of art, we assume that "every style is peculiar to a period of a culture, and that, in a given culture or epoch of cultures, there is only one style or a limited range of styles" (for *culture* read *specialty*); "works in the style of one time could not have been produced in another."[15]

The producers in the knowledge industry differ greatly in productivity and importance. A few individuals and teams are enormously productive and productive of work thought highly important by their peers. Larger numbers are regular producers of smaller quantities of material thought of some value by their peers. A very much larger number produce little, and perhaps most of that is generally thought of not much importance. It is abundantly clear from numerous studies how extremely skewed is the distribution of producers in terms both of volume and of importance of contribution to knowledge.[16] From our point of view, productivity and importance of output are significant especially as they affect the authority and influence of different producers. It is the great producers of high-quality work who have the greatest claims to cognitive authority both for other members of their specialties and for outsiders. The intellectual leaders of a field (not necessarily the same as the political or administrative leaders) are those recognized by their co-workers as the sources of exceptionally high-quality work and lots of it; the industry leaders are easy to recognize.[17] A low producer may indeed have great cognitive authority, known by personal recommendation and reputation to be a keen critic or analyst or perhaps a perfectionist who will not publish what does not satisfy his highest requirements. And a vigorous producer may have a mediocre reputation and little authority. But these are exceptions to the general rule: the industry leaders are the big producers of work recognized as of high quality.[18] They are the winners of the struggle for recognition of cognitive authority inside their specialty groups.

Knowledge Production and Quality Control

The aim of work in the knowledge industry is to make contributions to knowledge, but any particular publication may be a contribution to knowledge without being a contribution of knowledge. Naively, one might suppose that at least in the natural sciences each piece of published work represented a finding of permanent validity that was added to an inventory of knowledge, but this is not so. "Only a small proportion of the information contributed to science by research is eventually incorporated permanently in the body of scientific knowledge."[19] Even in physics, the exemplary hard science, much of what is published is rejected or simply ignored—Ziman says as much as 90 percent.[20] There are crowds of papers erroneously reporting "discoveries" that others cannot confirm, observations that others cannot reproduce, hypotheses and conjectures that persuade no one, flawed experiments that others cannot trust. Comments like this are common: "According to the majority of participants, the number of unsubstantiated claims prevalent at this time was overwhelming . . . .The young field of hypothalamic pituitary physiology is already littered with dead and dying hypotheses.' "[21]

Current controversies occupy much space in the learned journals. It is not only in philosophy that much published work consists of counterarguments, rebuttals, and refutations. A geologist remarks that "long controversies established a pattern in geology of essentially formal debate as a substitute for problem solving."[22] Reviews of what has been claimed on various sides of questions, reappraisals of old views, reconsiderations of positions, proposals for new terminology or new classifications, rehearsals of ancient questions: these share space with reports of observation and experiment. Works of criticism (literary, art, social and the like) may contribute to understanding and appreciation but are unlikely candidates for classification as contributions of knowledge. Much of the work published in the humanities "consists of mere exercises in the arts of opinion: explications of poems, novels or plays; descriptions or speculations about recurring themes, symbols, and psychological preoccupations, in the visual as well as the literary arts; efforts to construct a critical vocabulary, followed by still other efforts to dismantle it; and so on."[23] Not all published work makes contributions to knowledge; still less of it makes contributions of knowledge.

There is a fairly significant exception to this general claim about knowledge production. Almost any piece of work done in the industry that reports particular observations can be taken as making contributions of knowledge. An observational report can be construed in a weak sense as claiming that the investigator thinks he noted that so many people answered yes when asked a simple yes-or-no question or that he noted that a measuring instrument registered a particular reading at a particular time. Such small observational reports fill the literature and might generally be accepted as trustworthy (though inquirers have been known to manufacture or misrepresent their most elementary observation). But insofar as one suspects no fraud and believes the investigator is competent, the small elementary observational data he reports can be assumed to be correct, thus closing the question as to what was observed at the time. This is knowledge, but knowledge of an intrinsically uninteresting sort. It is interesting only relative to the more general conclusions drawn from the individual data. If elementary observational reports provided intrinsically valuable knowledge, we could all contribute valuable knowledge by reporting how many quarts of milk we consumed in the week and how many yellow automobiles we noticed on our way to work. When we ask whether the knowledge industry produces knowledge, we really do not want to ask whether its workers correctly report their elementary observations but whether they can make something interesting and valuable of their observations. Mere data collection is not what we are interested in.

Rather than viewing published works as contributions of knowledge, it seems better to consider them as constituting the public conversation of members of different communities of specialists, wherein proposals are made and sometimes ignored entirely, sometimes accepted, sometimes countered by different proposals, sometimes modified and accepted in the modified form. In effect, the audience for most work in the industry consists exclusively of the other specialists in the same sort of work. If the specialty is a large one, the audience will be large; if it is a small one, the audience will be tiny. "If you find three people reading your paper you feel flattered," says a mathematician.[24] In solo specialties, there may literally be no audience for particular publications; the solo specialist is a group with a single member and talks only to himself. Of course, there are plenty of publications addressed to larger audiences, but these are generally derivative from and dependent on those addressed to specialists. (A work with too large and unspecialized an audience is in danger of being considered nonscholarly.)

Out of the public conversation consisting of published papers and books, and what is probably more important, out of the private conversation and reflection that goes on in the various communities, knowledge sometimes emerges. The way a publication contributes to knowledge, if it does, is by changing the collective opinion of the specialist group. The size of a contribution is measured (not really, for we are not dealing with measurable quantities) by the size of the change produced in the collective opinion. Producing knowledge is not something the individual can do. All one can do is make proposals to the group and hope that they will be accepted in some form. If they are, and if the proposal is accepted by the group as settling some question for the time being, then a crucial step toward a contribution of knowledge has been made. If the proposal is taken simply as yet another opinion on the matter, then although no contribution of knowledge has been made, the situation of the group has been changed, for it now has a new proposal in its inventory of alternatives. If the proposal is ignored or forgotten and does nothing to change collective opinion, then no matter how certain the individual is that he has settled the question he addressed, he has not done so (except for himself).

Many proposals go unheeded. Not everyone is listening to everything said; not everyone takes the trouble to consider and evaluate what is said and come to a settled opinion on its value. And when all are attentively listening, they may disagree over the value of what they hear. As long as they disagree, questions remain open. They are closed, at least for the time being, only when the group comes to a general agreement that the matter is settled. This may happen without more than one or two of them actually giving careful consideration to particular publications. One individual may undertake to review the situation with respect to some question and produce a critical evaluation of various contributions that is accepted by others on the authority of the reviewer. In such a way, the reviewer may actually form public opinion in the specialist community, others being willing to take his word on the value of a contribution. On questions the community considers important, collective opinion will be likely to be easy to determine. On minor questions, it may not be at all clear what the group's opinion actually is. For outsiders to the group, it may be uncertain what the group's opinion is even on major questions. Research workers seem reluctant to write down accounts of the current state of opinion for general consumption.[25] Still, it is only by having an effect on public opinion in a specialized group that one can actually affect the state of knowledge, for insofar as we can identify the state of knowledge, it is only by looking to public opinion in some relevant group. Even this will not be enough, however, for the collective opinion of a group will constitute the state of knowledge in an area only for those who regard the specialty as having exclusive jurisdiction over the matter and as competent to settle questions in their sphere.

Individual publications may fail entirely to contribute to knowledge or may contribute to it without containing contributions of knowledge. They may move the group discussion forward, though nothing of what they say is recognizable in the final collective result. An account of the current state of knowledge on some particular topic generally will not be a simple enumeration of the separate contents of the separate original papers. It might have to ignore most of them and might have to give a much modified account of the content of those that remained. And of course there might be no knowledge to report but rather a mass of conflicting opinions: no closed questions, only open ones. Even when knowledge has resulted from inquiry, the worst place to look for a statement of what has been found is in the original publications representing individual attempts at knowledge production. One must look for an authoritative review and summary of the situation.

This account of knowledge production may seem outrageous to many people. How can knowledge be a matter of public opinion, even the public opinion of a group of specialists? This makes knowledge something subjective, whereas we should surely be able to see that a person can make a real discovery of important truth even though it is unrecognized as such by anyone else, and certainly what is accepted within a specialist group at a particular time may be false, whether or not recognized as such at a later time, and hence not really knowledge at all—for nothing can be called knowledge if it is not true.[26] Group consensus does not guarantee truth, hence it does not suffice to constitute knowledge. We should think of the production of knowledge as an objective matter. A person has made a contribution of knowledge if he has come to some true conclusion in a logically or methodologically correct way, and whether this has happened must not depend on what any other person or group happens to think has happened.

Such an objection is understandable but futile. Naturally when members of a group come to agreement on what they take to close a question, they think they have a true conclusion properly arrived at. They are not going to take anything as settling a question if they think it false or improperly arrived at. The problem for them and for anyone else is: what we can take to be true and properly arrived at. What can we hold to be known? It is to no purpose to say, "Don't hold anything to be known that is false or improperly arrived at." No one means to do that. Everyone will grant that today's views and verdicts may be revised tomorrow and that today's rejection of a proposal may be reversed tomorrow by enthusiastic acceptance. And still later the group may conclude that their original view was right. Our interest is in how we arrive at what we take for knowledge at a particular time. If someone objects that a conclusion we take for knowledge is mistaken or improperly arrived at, we can consider the objection and the proposed alternatives, if any; but then we are faced with the same question: Which of these alternatives can we take for knowledge?

The objection does, however, reflect a valid point: recognition that a group has produced some knowledge is not just recognition that the group has come to an agreement. It requires that we hold the view that the group is competent to settle questions in their domain. What we take for knowledge is not just a matter of public opinion and not just a matter of consensus of expert opinion. Expert opinion can constitute knowledge only for those who think the experts competent, who recognize them as having cognitive authority.

Professions generally aim to get and keep a monopoly on the right to criticize their own work by claiming that outsiders are incompetent to judge the merits and defects of their work. Specialties in the knowledge industry tend to behave as independent professions in this respect, and the peer review system, the cornerstone of the system of quality control in the industry, enshrines the principle of professional monopoly on criticism. Papers submitted for publication in learned journals and grant proposals are evaluated by other members of the specialty, who also review academic appointments and promotions. Members of related specialties may also participate. The boundaries of specialties being more or less vague, it may be unclear whether those doing the evaluation are members of the same or only of closely related specialties. But the basic principle is that only insiders, and outsiders who are almost insiders, evaluate the work produced in a specialty.

Given the fact that the industry consists of a large number of people working in a large number of relatively small specialty groups, it is natural to wonder if different groups do not have and apply quite different standards of evaluation, and if even within a single group there might not be different standards applied by different individuals or groups. Or is there a single set of standards uniformly applied across the entire industry? Michael Polanyi has argued that evaluation does go according to uniform standards, not across the entire range of activities we are investigating, but across the whole range of the natural sciences.[27] Although no one scientist has a sound understanding of more than a tiny portion of science, each scientist ordinarily can serve as a competent judge of work closely related to his own specialty. He will apply the same standards that he applies to his own specialty. All members of a specialty will apply the same standards; everyone is competent to judge related work; and so all of science will be covered by overlapping neighborhoods, and uniformity of standards will prevail. This argument is not persuasive. Polanyi does not show that members of the same specialty do indeed apply the same standards to work within their own specialty, or that when one judges work in a neighboring specialty, the standards one uses are the same as those used by insiders in that specialty. He rather seems simply to assume that they do.

Even if neighboring specialists did share the same standards, this would not ensure uniformity across all of science. "Having the same standards" does not mean "Having exactly the same reaction to all possible pieces of work." If it did mean that, few people would ever share standards or know if they did. Standards of evaluation are nothing remotely like exact procedures; people who are said to share standards are simply people whose evaluations resemble each other fairly closely. But if A's standards resemble B's fairly closely, and B's resemble C's fairly closely, A's need not resemble C's fairly closely. The more links in such a chain, the greater the possible differences between standards at opposite ends. The neighborhood principle—that one is competent to judge work done in one's immediate neighborhood as well as within one's own area—is compatible with gross variations in standards from area to area. In fact, it seems likely that even within a specialty, considerable disagreement about standards of evaluation is to be expected. A study of the peer review system found substantial disagreement among reviewers of grant proposals, who were all drawn from the specialty within which the proposal fell, and concluded that "the great bulk of reviewer disagreement observed is probably a result of real and legitimate differences of opinion among experts about what good science is or should be . . . contrary to a widely held belief that science is characterized by wide agreement about what is good work, who is doing good work, and what are promising lines of inquiry."[28] And who would seriously suppose that uniformity of standards, even if it existed in natural science, extended to cover all the humanities and social sciences as well? Acceptance of the principle of professional monopoly on criticism in effect means allowing each group to set its own standards, with no assurance that these will resemble those of other groups or that the group will agree on a set of standards.

If insiders are the ones primarily responsible for exercising quality control over work in their specialty, still they have to convince others that they are capable of fulfilling that responsibility. Monopolies on criticism have to be won and constantly justified. For outsiders, the question is whether what the insiders declare to be newly produced knowledge can be taken as such. It is true that outsiders may have no occasion to raise such questions; the industry may for long periods of time go on with the various specialties and fields largely ignoring each other, each operating as an independent world of its own. But any outsider who wants or needs to use the products of a specialty has to be sure that the products will bear using, that they are trustworthy. Any outsider who has to decide which specialties to support has to decide which are worth supporting , and cannot simply take the word of the insiders as settling the question of the value of their enterprise.[29] For one thing, the familiar egocentric illusion leads people to overestimate the value and importance of their own specialties. This almost inescapable form of illusion is just as common in the knowledge industry as elsewhere in life. But beyond that is the possibility that a specialty or entire field that the insiders all agree to be highly productive of valuable new knowledge will seem to be nothing of the sort to the outside observer. If the same standards were indeed applied everywhere in the knowledge industry, this would not be a serious possibility. Given that everyone inclines to overvalue his own work, application of uniform standards would not lead to such drastic misevaluations, with insiders seeing important contributions to knowledge where outsiders using the same standards saw only futile time wasting. But if standards differ widely from area to area in the industry, then the possibility exists that some branches of the industry might be vigorously and successfully producing knowledge while other branches were producing no knowledge or none of value.

Why suppose that every sort of inquiry in which people engage should be successful? Why suppose that, at a particular time, all the subjects that interest people are amenable to systematic inquiry? In fact plenty of branches of the knowledge industry are found, by outside observers and by insiders as well, to produce nothing of value, however well the work produced meets the standards accepted within a specialty. Poor work is done in all fields, as judged by internal standards; that is not the issue. The issue is whether there are specialties that produce nothing of value, as judged by other standards. The pseudo-sciences are excluded from the knowledge-producing establishment of university departments and federally supported research agencies because outsiders are unconvinced that they are productive of knowledge at all. But even within the establishment, the claims of many fields to be productive of knowledge are often challenged. "Much could be gained by eliminating current practice as well as adding to it. For much of current social science is a waste of time, and someone needs to say so."[30] A philosopher critic claimed that "pure research in social psychology is among the most unproductive fields of human endeavor today."[31] Many social psychologists came to share that view: "Experimental social psychology can never be serious."[32] A reviewer commenting on the "extreme crisis verging on collapse" within academic linguistics noted the "endless monographs, articles, counter-articles, replies and rejoinders in a thousand reviews designed to perpetuate . . . Byzantine debates. This lavishly financed abuse . . . is of course endemic to the humanities and social sciences at large."[33] These are not complaints of the sort one might hear in any field—that too much work is published that is trivial, flawed, hasty, and so forth. Even the most successful fields have their shares of poor work, despite the efforts of the peer-review quality control system. Rather, these are complaints about entire specialties and fields that seem flourishing to the insiders but barren to outsiders.

Assuming that one was persuaded that the negative criticism was justified, one might wonder how that unproductive production could continue. If production was continued only so long as outsiders found the results to be of use, then such negative criticism, if widespread, presumably would lead to cessation of production or drastic alteration in production methods. But in fact production in the knowledge industry does not depend uniformly or strongly on outsiders' perception of utility. Work continues because groups of specialists still want to work in a particular line and find the necessary support. Even if an insider agrees that the work is of little value, he may want to continue because of inertia, inability, or unwillingness to find a different line of work to pursue, the academic's need to find things for doctoral students to do, the need to continue publishing to maintain and enhance one's reputation, and the continuing ability to gain reputation by work that one privately admits to be of doubtful value, and for other creditable and discreditable reasons.[34] But groups of specialists can maintain enthusiasm for a style of work even in the face of severe external criticism, asserting their monopoly on serious evaluation of their own work. Since research in the public sector is not supported by sale of its products, other support must be found. That support may be almost automatic and routine for long periods of time. Much research, especially in academic institutions, is what one could call sheltered research; basic support is guaranteed by the tenure system. Academic tenure is a guarantee of freedom to pursue a line of work simply because one wants to do so. The fact that outsiders find such work trivial and fruitless does not constitute a sufficient reason for its discontinuance, if the work is inexpensive to do and if the major need is time in which to do it. So long as appointments and promotions depend largely on the opinions of peers, and so long as there are peers ready to testify to the merit of a person's work, appointments will continue to be made, tenure granted, and freedom to pursue self-selected projects guaranteed, even when for outsiders, the peers called on to evaluate each others' work are collectively pursuing a useless line of activity. Expensive work, requiring large support staffs or costly equipment or both, naturally requires that producers convince someone outside their specialty to provide the money. If the funders rely exclusively or mainly on peer evaluations, the results can be the same as for inexpensive and sheltered research. Not every would-be specialist group gets entrenched in the shelter of academia or in the eligibility lists of large funding agencies, and outside funding agencies for quite accidental reasons may find themselves forced to abandon exclusive or heavy reliance on peer evaluations of the worth of their own work. But when money is freely available, every entrenched respectable specialty may get support for work that outside critics think valueless. As long as someone with money to give in support of research is still persuaded of the value of a specialty, either because he thinks the specialty is producing worthwhile knowledge or because he is optimistic that it will ultimately begin to do so, the work can go on, however much derided by critics. Every outsider has to arrive at his own conclusion about whether a specialist group is or is not producing something of value, and while some outsiders reject a specialty as nonproductive, others may see exactly the same results as well worth support. The question how unproductive production can continue becomes the question why the supporters still think production worth support, a question that might have the most various answers.

Fashion and Intellectual Taste

While production can go on whether or not it is generally recognized as being the production of knowledge, it does not long go on in the same way. Research styles change constantly, though not at a uniform rate throughout the industry. New areas to explore continue to be found; new ways of exploring them continue to be devised. Specialties do not last forever; they grow and decline, the volume of production swelling and then diminishing to a trickle. New specialties arise, old specialty lines converge and diverge, changing style of approach in small or large ways, transforming the character of work done slightly or massively. How are we to think of this constant change? As the continual discovery of improved ways of conducting inquiry and of richer ores of potential knowledge to be mined? As constant improvement in methods of production and volume of knowledge produced? Or perhaps as a restless search for something that will work, as rejection of unproductive old ways for what may turn out to be unproductive new ways?

Let us reflect on the extent of the changes in the character of work done in the knowledge industry, taking illustrations from the social sciences and humanities. History provides a convenient example.[35] Old and new ways of doing history look different even to the casual observer. The old way produces narratives, the new produces analyses; the old focuses on events, the new, on conditions and changes of conditions. The old concentrates on the actions of a few prominent actors; the new dwells on the life of the many and poor. The old is literary in style of presentation; the new is likely to be quantitative and abstract. One accustomed to the old style hardly recognizes work in the new style as history at all.

Analogous comparisons of old and new styles of work could be made in any of the humanities and social sciences, with similar results. One might compare work done in philosophy under the banners of logical positivism, then ordinary language philosophy; in literary criticism, the rise and fall of the New Criticism, the subsequent ascendancies of structuralism, poststructuralism, deconstruction; work in linguistics before and after the appearance of Noam Chomsky; the growth of behavioral and quantitative approaches in political science and sociology, and the more recent growth of interpretive social science; the mathematization of economics; the transformation of geography into a social science. The big changes are evident on the most superficial examination of older and newer work. To an older generation, the new work may seem to be not work in the same field at all: not really philosophy, not really history.[36] Major changes seem to alter radically the very nature of the field of study, making it unrecognizably different from what it was. A thousand less drastic but significant changes in objects, means, and results can be discovered by closer stylistic analysis. Radical changes in aims and methods have been accompanied by conflict sometimes amounting to open warfare, with campaigns to capture academic departments, editorships of journals, and offices in professional associations, seats of power in the world of academic research. Such episodes are inevitably called revolutions, and no doubt they are. They are certainly not examples of simple technological progress. They are stylistic revolutions. What explains them?

The idea of fashion is the key element in an answer. In economics, writes Jacob Viner, "There is a constant dialectic between the empirical and rationalistic approaches. It has never been settled except on the basis of changing intellectual fashions. . . . 'fashion' must be appealed to, to explain the temporary dominance of either approach."[37] Reviews, surveys, and general discussions of research are studded with allusions to fashion:

"There are signs that obscurity is becoming fashionable in Oxford philosophy."[38] "Fashion itself cast a long shadow over the new enterprise of urban history."[39] "Fashion and standards in political science changed more than once between the Great Depression and the postwar period, once again . . . during the behavioral 1950s, and are undergoing another."[40] "The real bond that makes them seem alike is that they are all works of critical high fashion."[41] "In academic work the evaluation of concepts depends as much upon fashion as upon utility."[42] "Were we getting closer to the truth, or just drifting in the tides of critical fashion?"[43] To some it seems obvious that we must appeal to fashion to explain change: "Who does not know that 'fashion' and 'mode' rule our life?"[44]

The great philosopher-sociologist Georg Simmel thought that the rule of fashion in such important matters as science would be unendurable.[45] Hagstrom thinks that fashion in science represents deviance from scientific ideals.[46] To label something with the tag of fashion is, for many people, a debunking tactic; "merely fashionable" is a phrase of contemptuous dismissal. Fashion is both trivial and irrational.[47] Can we accept an explanation of change that discredits what it explains? Could so frivolous a thing as fashion really be behind major changes in so solemn an enterprise as scholarly production?

Our earlier discussion of style has prepared the ground for an examination of the claims of fashion. Fashion in general, and intellectual fashion in particular, are best thought of as matters of style. From the outside, fashion is a matter of the temporary popularity of a new stylistic feature or complex of features. What is fashionable may be a whole style, an entire way of working, or just a detail of a way of working: a new procedure, concept, tool, style of argument, problem area. New stylistic variants appear constantly, some large and distinctive, most small and inconspicuous. Some spread among a population of research workers until almost everyone has adopted them; most are not adopted by anyone except the originator. How they arise is not a question to be answered by appeal to fashion—that is for the theory of invention and creativity to worry about.

Fashion enters when we try to explain the widespread adoption of a stylistic variant. At the most superficial level, however, fashion is no explanation but rather a surface phenomenon that is to be explained. The fate of a stylistic innovation can be traced over time, and its rise and fall depicted in graphic terms. We can count the numbers of people who adopt the innovation, measure the time it takes for the innovation to be adopted, tabulate the numbers of books and articles exhibiting use of the innovation, draw curves showing rise and fall in utilization, and supply mathematical formulas that describe the shape of the curves. At this most superficial level, we can distinguish fads (rapidly and widely adopted and quickly dropped, curves with sharp rises and falls) from fashions (more slowly adopted, more slowly abandoned) from newly born conventions or customs (slowly adopted, widely accepted for a long time). A fashion is, from the outside, simply a widely but temporarily employed stylistic innovation.

Beneath the surface, fashion involves change of taste.[48] A currently fashionable style especially appeals to the current taste. When a new style comes into fashion, an older style becomes old-fashioned and outmoded. Last year's clothing is put away not because it is worn out but because present taste finds it unattractive and unwearable. Last year's research style is abandoned for a new one not because nothing more could be done in the old style but because further work in that style now seems tedious, trivial, stale, pointless, or, in more extreme shifts of taste, misdirected, foolish, ridiculous, contemptible. What was previously attractive comes to be unattractive; what would earlier have been unattractive and even bizarre comes to seem attractive. Taste changes and turns against what it had previously favored. Change of taste may precede change of style. One's current style loses its appeal, and one looks around for a more attractive style. Change of style may precede change of taste: one tries working in a new style even though at first it seems awkward and repulsive, then gradually comes to think it natural and superior to the old style it has replaced. Change of taste need not be confined to those actually using or working in a style. If one's style of work changes, one hopes that the taste of members of one's audience will also change, and in the same direction. Changes of taste can be small or large. Those that occur in revolutionary times are large, but tastes are probably shifting slightly all the time.

The notion of taste is familiar enough, but the specific notion of intellectual taste may need further comment. Description of one's intellectual taste is description of how one is prone to criticize, evaluate, and appreciate the intellectual work one does oneself or others do.[49] It is intellectual taste showing itself when one finds oneself feeling that, for example, a piece of work is too abstract or too immersed in trivial detail, too loosely argued or unnecessarily explicit, directed at basically trivial questions or at deeply interesting ones. It is intellectual taste that judges the intrinsic interest of problems and solutions, the appropriateness of ways of approaching problems, the sufficiency or insufficiency of a treatment of a problem. One's explicitly formulated standards are reflections of one's intellectual taste. When one tries to state the criteria or principles behind particular judgments, one is trying to give expression to one's taste. But explicit standards, criteria, and principles are usually, if not always, imperfect reflections of taste. This is easily shown. Perhaps the archetypal expression of taste is a judgment that such and such is enough: important enough to merit attention, well enough organized, strongly enough supported by the evidence, presented in enough detail, carefully enough worked out. Attempts to settle questions of "enoughness" by appeal to explicit standards often are total failures. We may be certain that such and such is enough but unable to formulate an explicit rule for general use that would parallel the verdicts of our intellectual taste. Taste is no judge of the truth or falsity of statements but of the adequacy of the work done to get to a particular statement and of the interest or importance, not the truth, of the statement. Shifts of intellectual taste are shifts in what one thinks it is good to know and in what one thinks is a good way of getting to know it, in what one thinks is worth doing and in what one thinks is the best way to do it.

When we see that an individual or a group has changed its style of work in some degree—adopted a new technique, borrowed a new concept—we cannot tell without further inquiry whether any change of taste has occurred. We need two different categories for the phenomena that on the surface are cases of fashion. We will call them first-degree fashions if no change of taste is involved, and second-degree fashions if change of taste is involved. Without trying to say how one tells which is which, we can see that there must be plenty of cases of first-degree fashions: novelties whose value or utility can be judged on already established criteria, new tools or techniques that are more efficient or effective than old ones, new questions asked because there is money available to pay for answering them, or because they are easier to answer than others. Changes in methods respond to changes in the external environment (which offers new tools, new financial or practical incentives, and so on), as well as to changes of taste. Much of the short-term, day-to-day change in research style probably can be safely assigned to the category of first-degree fashion. So can many changing evaluations of other people's specialties or one's own. Progress slows down or speeds up in a field. We think we are doing worse or better now than we were a few years ago and may think so because our bases of evaluation are stable but objective conditions have changed or because objective conditions are the same but our bases of evaluation have changed. It can be difficult to tell which is the actual situation.

One reason often given to explain the decline or disappearance of a specialty line is the exhaustion of research opportunities in the specialty—that is, the increasing difficulty of discovering interesting problems for research that can be approached with available techniques.[50] A style of work that once seemed productive comes to seem exhausted of its potentialities. A new and more productive style is sought that will lead to renewed growth in the old specialty or even the formation of a new specialty. The notion of the exhaustion of a style does seem a plausible explanation of change. When most of what can be done within a style has been done, when the future of the present executants is being cramped by the hold of the past, when "original imagination faces a dead end," the time is ripe for stylistic change.[51] But appeal to exhaustion of a style is often inconclusive and unsatisfactory. To the outsider, a research style may have been exhausted from the start, while to the insider, it may seem far from exhausted. At some point, producers may come to feel dissatisfied with the "distressing triviality" of their findings, as those who worked for years in the psychological specialty of verbal learning apparently did.[52] But findings may have been distressingly trivial for a long time before insiders came to feel they were, and the last crumbs of information yielded may look no smaller than the first crumbs. When the same kind of work that last year seemed exciting now seems distressingly trivial, we may suspect not that the supply of real potentialities has been reduced but that taste has changed.

There is still a deeper question to face, if not to answer with much confidence. What explains changes of taste? Two kinds of explanation are available. As writers on fashion in other realms of human affairs often stress, fashion has force; it exercises a social compulsion.[53] We may suppose that this is true as well in the spread of an intellectual fashion of the second degree. The taste of many changes because that of others has changed, and in response to that change. Those who first adopt a new style are drawn to it; those who last adopt it are more nearly driven away from an earlier style. As more and more people's taste changes, those whose taste has not yet changed find themselves under more and more pressure to yield. As we come to believe that everyone else now finds unsuitable or even ridiculous what we are still doing, we are likely to feel more pressure to stop doing it and are more likely to come to share their views. The pressure we feel need involve no overt actions or words from others; it is not that they urge us to change or threaten us with retribution if we fail to change. It is simply that we think we know what they are thinking about us.

Our change of taste is not conscious and deliberate imitation of others. One can indeed deliberately decide to imitate a style of work or try to like a new style, but one cannot simply decide to like it. One can cynically adopt a fashion and pretend to like it while secretly despising it; that is a different case. Succumbing to fashion is not, as some have said, simply doing what others do, or simply doing what others do because one sees them doing it. It is coming to prefer a new style, from the unconscious influence on one's own taste of recognition of others' changes of taste. Since it depends on recognition of others' changes of taste, it also depends on the number and speed of propagation, of signs of changing tastes, and on individual sensitivity to the signs. Those who are so positioned as to be most aware of others' changes of taste will feel its force soonest, while those who are out of communication with the group will feel it last.

This is fashion as a mass phenomenon: the greater the number of those whose taste changes, the greater the pressure to change. The numbers of people involved in a sector of the knowledge industry is not likely to be so large as to qualify as a mass, but the pressure of numbers may still be significant. Clearly some people, particularly those with cognitive authority, carry more weight than others. The more cognitive authority an individual is recognized as having, the more likely it is that the authority's apparent changes of taste will lead to changes in one's own taste. Cognitive authority can extend over any question of value, and intellectual taste is a matter of intellectual values. If my authority says that we have been mistakenly intolerant of this new way of working and overly satisfied with our old way of working, then I am likely to reflect that maybe we have been overly satisfied and that the new style does deserve to be taken seriously. And then I may find, after reflection, that my taste is shifting. A cognitive authority can be a fashion leader in that others come to admire the same thing as that person because that person has come to admire it, and because they give great weight to his views and preferences. An innovation made by one with no particular authority will not become fashionable unless taken up by those who do have authority, who legitimize the innovation, making it acceptable for others to try and exerting an influence that may lead others to try. But if fashion leaders facilitate the acceptance of a novelty, they have no irresistible power over others' taste. They may find themselves without followers. Here as in other sorts of cognitive authority, there may be inner obstacles to acceptance of the word or example of the authority. The authority who begins to tell us stories we find hopelessly implausible will lose authority rather than gain a follower, and the authority who recommends a style of inquiry that we find hopelessly *outré* may discredit himself rather than gain a follower.

Both the influence of cognitive authorities and the influence of sheer numbers have to be appealed to in order to account for widespread changes of taste, but the tastes of a group may also change even though no individual's taste changes. The predominant style of work in a group might change either because old members suffered a change of taste or because new workers coming in to the group had different tastes. If a group is invaded by new members coming from a different research area, bringing with them already formed and different tastes, then the average taste of a group might change over time though no individual's taste changed. More commonly, new recruits to the group might acquire from their teachers what was previously a minority taste, so that as older members of the group dropped out, what had been a minority taste became a majority taste. This is perhaps a standard generation-gap method of change, though it assumes that at least some of the older generation decisively influenced the younger generation. These would be the cognitive authorities who failed to influence their contemporaries but had great influence as teachers. Another sort of generation gap might arise from a spontaneous collective revulsion among the young against the entire older generation, the young denying all cognitive authority to the elders and reacting to and acting on each other to form a new collective taste. No doubt this only begins to categorize the devious and hidden routes through which taste changes occur.

Changes of taste cannot be compelled, neither can they be predicted. Tarde's question,"Why, given one hundred different innovations conceived of at the same time, . . . ten will spread abroad, while ninety will be forgotten," is no closer to being answered now than when he posed it a century ago. It is unlikely to be answered, if as an answer one demanded a sure way of telling in advance which ten would succeed.[54]

Fashion In The Knowledge Industry

Now we have a better idea of how styles of inquiry might change. Can we agree that there are fashions in research? Undoubtedly there are in the superficial sense of first-degree fashions.[55] Styles of inquiry certainly do change; topics, tools, and procedures have their ups and downs in popularity. The serious question is whether stylistic changes involve changes of taste. It has been denied that they do, at least in the natural sciences. Thomas Kuhn thinks that the criteria or values used in theory choice in the natural sciences (which would be expressions of intellectual taste) are "fixed once and for all," roughly speaking, "but only very roughly."[56] He quickly admits that the actual application of those values (for example, of accuracy, scope, simplicity), and more clearly the relative weights attached to different criteria, vary markedly with time and also with field of application. But this is inconclusive, for choice among theories is only one sort of manifestation of intellectual taste, and there are plentiful signs of changes of taste in other areas. Here is an example:

In the great post-Darwinian revival of zoology it was believed by nearly all serious biologists that the really important task was to annotate in ever-increasing detail the course of evolution. In those bad old days quite a number of biological disciplines were thought to achieve respectability for the first time when it became possible to describe them as "comparative.". . . In the reaction against comparative anatomy, comparative physiology became an equally great—or even worse— nuisance. Comparative anatomy being now discredited, the foremost obligation of zoologists was thought to be an understanding of the physiology of lower animals. Much of this work was very dull and unilluminating. . . . Unhappily, it seems to be of the nature of academic revolutions to become an abuse before their pretentions are finally repudiated with a kind of weary disgust.[57]

To the outsider that sounds like a description of changing taste. However it is with the natural sciences, the human studies are readily viewed as mounted on the whirligig of taste. In almost any field of the human studies, one might sometime say with Lynn White that "our studies have arrived at a point where scholars are beginning to ask entirely new kinds of questions, are tackling almost unknown types of material to extract evidence, and are finding intellectual satisfaction in sorts of answers which our ancestors would have regarded as lunacy."[58] The last clause is the crucial one: the sources of intellectual satisfaction change. We suffer radical losses of satisfaction: "We are having this session on 'Rethinking Anthropology' because many of us are. . . sick of anthropology as it is exemplified in most of our journals, books, and courses—even those we have ourselves perpetrated."[59] We come to think of the things our colleagues are doing as "the scrapings and shavings of historical antiquarianism, . . . the rehashing over and over again of the same tired old questions."[60] Correspondingly, we discover new enthusiasms and find ourselves valuing new kinds of things. Everyone who has worked in a university environment for more than a few years is likely to have witnessed such changes in others and to have undergone such changes personally. The longer one stays, the more unavoidable the signs of constant change of intellectual taste. "It is ever varying, not merely among the masses of men, but in the individual man. The wind of taste bloweth where it listeth; you can no more tell why it changes, or what will be its next manifestation, than you can say why the crinoline came in or why it went out. . . . A taste appears, and often runs through the world like a prairie fire; the matter that has kindled it is too small to be detected, and when it ceases to blaze you cannot tell what has put it out."[61]

Changes of intellectual taste, small and large, are almost undeniable; the same cannot be said for the proposed mechanism of change. Scientists and scholars are not supposed to change their underlying standards or intellectual taste in response to awareness of others' changing tastes. They are supposed to be responsive solely to valid argument and compelling evidence. It looks as if we were claiming that scholars and scientists, like other people in other situations, are prone to jump on bandwagons; it looks as if change of intellectual taste was "irrational, a matter for mob psychology."[62] If, as the sociologist Blumer insists, fashion is "not guided by utilitarian or rational considerations . . . the pretended merit or value of competing models cannot be demonstrated through open and decisive test," then irrationality lies at the heart of the whole enterprise of knowledge production.[63]

There is, however, a striking exception to the ideology of imperviousness to personal influence: the stage of formal education of the future research worker. It is a, if not the, principal point of graduate education to form the taste of the future researcher. Unless the student can be brought to develop a proper intellectual taste, he has not been socialized and cannot be trusted to do independent work. It is not assumed that the student already has a correct sense of what constitutes a significant problem or an appropriate way of approaching it. The student is to develop a taste consistent with those of the teachers, and it is not frowned upon for the student to take the teacher as a model whose taste is to be emulated as far as possible. The objective provision of demonstrations of the superior merits of the teacher's way of doing things could not be the sole means of acquiring a correct taste. Before acquiring that taste, the student is not in a position to evaluate the demonstrations. The apprenticeship that is the ordinary route to independent status as a professional research worker is unlikely to work unless the student recognizes the master as having a high degree of cognitive authority, hence as having a properly high degree of influence on the student's mind.

If personal influence is allowed at this stage, ideology has it that it is supposed to be rigorously excluded after entrance into independent research. Why research workers should be supposed capable of such exclusion is a mystery, for they are provided with no techniques they might use to stay immune from unconscious influence of the opinions of others. And it is beyond belief that they are in fact indifferent to the opinions of their peers or that they should learn what the rest of humanity have not learned: how to escape the influence of one's milieu. Since we cannot realistically expect them to do what others cannot do, it should be no cause of scandal if we recognize personal influence as effective in changing the tastes of workers in the knowledge industry.[64]

Still, some might say, the crucial question is whether there are adequate reasons for changes of taste, whatever the unknown psychological influences may be that actually work on particular individuals. However changes of intellectual taste come about, we want assurances that they can be rationally justified; otherwise the foundations of the whole industry would be insecure. The industry cannot be based on inexplicable personal whim. The demand for adequate reasons in the area of basic taste is not so different from the demand for adequate basis for the acceptance of scientific theories expressed by J. O. Wisdom: "so long as you have a specific logical procedure as a basis, e.g. uniform evidence accepted by the top-grade people in the line, it does not affect the rationality or status of the theory if a lot of rank and file people . . . accept the theory mainly on sociological grounds."[65] It would be all right if the mob followed fashion as long as the leaders could provide satisfactory stories to justify the fashion they were following. But it is characteristic of changes of taste, intellectual as well as moral or aesthetic, that a specific logical procedure for justification of changes of taste is not available. We explain or justify adoption of a stylistic innovation by appeal to taste and its criteria and standards so far as expressible. If taste is unchanged during the adoption process, fashion in the deeper sense is not involved. If taste changes, then the innovation is justified by appeal to the new taste, not to the old, which would have rejected the innovation. But to what could one appeal in justifying a change of taste? Not the old taste; not some other taste that one does not share; and not the new taste itself. Fashion in the deeper sense involves movement to a new evaluative position, and any arguments for the move have to be logically inconclusive. It is pointless to demand that one do what cannot be done: give conclusive reasons for changes of taste.

Must we conclude that changes of taste are irrational and that the whole industry rests on irrational foundations? We may do so, but there is an alternative view. We can instead hold that changes of taste are neither rational nor irrational, that rationality itself has to be judged solely from within the framework provided by an intellectual taste. The force of Blumer's claim that fashion "is not guided by utilitarian or rational considerations" then becomes not an indictment of changes of mind and behavior that fail to conform to what they might have conformed to but rather an exhibition of the kind of change involved: a move into a new set of conditions for the play of utilitarian or rational considerations.

The proposed mechanism of change of taste may not be objectionable after all. But is there any evidence that it actually works to produce changes of taste? Since the mechanism is an unconscious one, we are not going to be able to answer the question by simple observation or introspection.[66] It is not even clear what sorts of evidence would be relevant to settling the question. But one sort of evidence that is relevant is in good supply: evidence of the social pressure that fashion involves. All of us can supply from our own experience information about what we would look down on and expect others to look down on. We could supply parallels to this: "If in reply to an inquiry from one of your colleagues concerning your current research interests, you said you were studying the Italian Constitutional Court, what do you suppose his reaction would be? He probably would regard you as a mossback institutionalist completely out of the mainstream of the discipline."[67]

Most of us have felt the push and pull of changes in others' notions of the most appropriate technique or procedure: "If Paris says wear it, wear it. Be certain to employ whichever statistical technique is taking Ann Arbor by storm this summer . . . . Having finally learned how to tell a *beta* from a *b*, political scientists reeled under the full force of the factor analysis offensive. Now, still scratching our heads over orthogonal versus oblique rotations, we're told that discriminant analysis is avant garde. What's next? Smart money is riding on canonical correlation ."[68] Any of us may have heard the rumors about what styles are in and what are on their way out: "Those of us who were graduate students in the thirties may recall how the word went around that colonial history was dead; no ambitious young graduate student would venture into that moribund field, and few then did. Intellectual history was the in thing. But we all know what has since happened to colonial history, while intellectual history is now in turn consigned to oblivion."[69] This is not proof, but it is evidence.

We may conclude, then, that production in the knowledge industry is in part explained by reference to fashion and underlying changes of intellectual taste. Fashion affects not only current production but also current estimates of past work. A change of taste can lead to virtual abandonment of past work; a community may reject its past and try to start over from the beginning with a clean slate. Or a specialty line may disappear entirely, the entire previous production left to gather dust on library shelves, completely ignored.

Fashion gives us a view of the obsolescence of research different from the stories usually offered to account for diminishing use of old scientific work. Original scientific research reports are no longer needed when their findings are replaced by better versions, or are rejected as incorrect, or are subsumed under new generalizations, or when they pass into the common knowledge of a field.[70] But a somewhat different fate comes to research outmoded by changes in taste. It is not that we reject the old answers to questions in favor of new answers; rather, we reject the old questions as misguided or trivial. The old work is forgettable, and no one is concerned to assign it any definite status in relation to the current body of knowledge. It is not part of what we now know, but also not part of what we now know to be false; it is just ignored.

The knowledge industry, then, on this account, consists of numerous shifting small groups of specialists, producing paper results meant to change the minds of their fellow specialists, evaluating each others' offerings according to different standards, which change unpredictably over time as intellectual taste changes. The paper results do not represent small contributions of knowledge. Most of them have little or no impact on the group conclusions that represent the candidates for acceptance as additions to the stock of knowledge. In any field, most of those pieces of paper may be considered of little value. In some fields, none of them may contribute to knowledge, for no knowledge may be forthcoming at all. The workers in the industry may be thought of as striving to acquire the largest possible degree of cognitive authority in the areas of their work.

This view of the industry is not an especially bright one. For the insiders, it may be discouraging to think, or admit, that what one does may have little or no effect on the state of knowledge. It is more comforting to think that a publication consists of a permanent, if small, contribution to the sum of knowledge in the form of a contribution of knowledge. For outsiders, it is disconcerting to think that armies of learned men and women might work at the production of knowledge and fail to produce any. It is alarming to hear that one can seriously say of a branch of this industry, "Not only have we not learned anything in the past thirty years, but we seem to have proceeded on premises which commonsense, logic, and available knowledge would declare to be most naive."[71] Certainly that cannot be said of the whole industry; but of which parts can it, or similar things, be said?

Reflection on fashion and intellectual taste raises a more profoundly unnerving question. Why should one be expected to put one's trust in an enterprise whose very foundations were subject to unpredictable and more or less drastic shifts of intellectual taste? It is one thing to recognize that views about the world are likely to change as new discoveries are made; it is quite another to recognize that they are likely to change not as new discoveries are made but as people's bases for judgment change. If one could have assurances that those changes were always for the better, one might be content; but it must be clear that to those whose taste changed, the changes will always seem to be for the better, and that there is no point in asking them for assurances. Today they are confidently pursuing this line, but how long will that last, and what might their line be tomorrow? The idea of fashion is often used to discredit; *merely fashionable* is a label meant to diminish what it is applied to. And it does appear that cognitive authority seems to weaken if one supposes that it rests on changeable intellectual taste. Inconsistency over time can be as unnerving as inconsistency at one time. And the larger and more rapid the changes of taste, the less weight one is likely to feel able to give to work that expresses that changeable taste. Authority diminishes when it comes to seem the authority of today's changeable fashion.

Notes

1. The popularity of the phrase *knowledge industry* is perhaps due to Fritz Machlup, whose *The Production and Distribution of Knowledge in the United States* (Princeton: Princeton University Press, 1962) was the first explicit economic analysis of knowledge production and distribution. Most of the components of his industry are concerned with distribution, not new production, of knowledge. The knowledge industry as defined for our purposes is only a sector, though certainly a central sector, of Machlup's knowledge industry: basic and applied research. A new version of the 1962 work is scheduled to appear in several volumes under the collective title *Knowledge: Its Creation, Distribution, and Economic Significance*. The first two volumes, now in print, are entitled *Knowledge and Knowledge Production* and *The Branches of Learning* (Princeton: Princeton University Press, 1980 and 1982, respectively). Machlup employs a wide concept of knowledge and defines knowledge production as "any human (or human-induced) activity effectively designed to create, alter, or confirm in a human mind a meaningful

apperception, awareness, cognizance, or consciousness of anything
whatsoever" (*Knowledge and Knowledge Production*, p. 92). On that definition, there is no question that the knowledge industry does indeed
produce knowledge. But that is an unusually generous definition, suitable for Machlup's purposes but not for ours.

2. Warren O. Hagstrom, "Traditional and Modern Forms of Scientific
Teamwork," *Administrative Science Quarterly* 9 (1964): 241-63.

3. On specialties, see Warren O. Hagstrom, *The Scientific Community*
(New York: Basic Books, 1965), Ch. 4, esp. pp. 159-63; Warren O.
Hagstrom, *Competition and Teamwork in Science*, Final Report to the National Science Foundation for Research Grant GS-657 to the University
of Wisconsin (Madison, 1967); Richard Whitley, "Cognitive and Social
Institutionalization of Scientific Specialties and Research Areas," in *Social Processes of Scientific Development*, ed. Richard Whitley (London:
Routledge & Kegan Paul, 1974), pp. 69-95; Daryl E. Chubin, "The Conceptualization of Scientific Specialties," *Sociological Quarterly* 17 (1976):
448-76.

4. Warren O. Hagstrom, "Competition in Science," *American Sociological Review* 39 (1974): 1-18.

5. Hagstrom, *Scientific Community*, p. 91; cf. Hagstrom, *Competition
and Teamwork in Science*.

6. *Biology and the Future of Man*, ed. Philip Handler (New York:
Oxford University Press, 1970), p. 523: "The number of groups of or-
ganisms is so great that frequently one man during his lifetime is the
only person investigating a particular group."

7. Karin D. Knorr-Cetina, *The Manufacture of Knowledge: An Essay on
the Constructivist and Contextual Nature of Science* (Oxford: Pergamon
Press, 1982), puts great stress on "variable transscientific fields" as
affecting scientific choice and reasoning, for example, sources of funding, publishers, and employers, as well as members of a specialty. Self-
selected work is usually financed by grants, other-selected work by
contracts. In Vollmer's formulation, "Grants support people so that
they can do certain kinds of work; contracts support work done according to agreed-upon specifications." Howard M. Vollmer, "The Organization of Basic and Applied Research," in *The Social Contexts of
Research*, ed. Saad Z. Nagi and Ronald G. Corwin (New York: Wiley-
Interscience, 1972), p. 82. But the relation between source of proposal
and form of funding can be much more complex. See Irving Louis
Horowitz and James Everett Katz, *Social Science and Public Policy in the
United States* (New York: Praeger, 1975), p. 148. Self-selected work is
likely to be pure research, other-selected work to be applied research,
but much self-selected work is applied, and a person working as part

of a team under someone else's direction may be working at pure research. See Roger G. Krohn, *The Social Shaping of Science: Institutions, Ideology, and Careers in Science* (Westport, Conn.: Greenwood Press, 1971), on support and control of research; also Simon Marcson, *The Scientist in American Industry: Some Organizational Determinants in Manpower Utilization* (New York: Industrial Relations Section, Department of Economics, Princeton University, 1960); Harvey Brooks, *The Government of Science* (Cambridge: MIT Press, 1968).

8. Bruno Latour and Steve Woolgar, *Laboratory Life: The Social Construction of Scientific Facts*, Sage Library of Social Research, vol. 80 (Beverly Hills: Sage, 1979), p. 71: "The production of papers is acknowledged by participants as the main objective of their activity."

9. This is close to Pierre Bourdieu's view, as expressed in his "The Specificity of the Scientific Field and the Social Conditions of the Progress of Reason," *Social Science Information* 14 (1975): 19-47. But he claims the object is "the monopoly of scientific authority, defined inseparably as technical capacity and social power, or, to put it another way, the monopoly of scientific competence, in the sense of a particular agent's socially recognized capacity to speak and act legitimately (i.e. in an authorized and authoritative way) in scientific matters" (p. 19). *Monopoly* seems too strong; does one really want to have all the cognitive authority, one's fellow specialists being without any at all? And one might have great authority without being an explicitly authorized spokesman for a group.

10. Jonathan R. Cole and Stephen Cole, *Social Stratification in Science* (Chicago: University of Chicago Press, 1973).

11. Theodore Caplow and Reece J. McGee, *The Academic Marketplace* (Garden City, N.Y.: Doubleday, Anchor Books, 1965), p. 110.

12. E. H. Gombrich, "Style," *International Encyclopedia of the Social Sciences* (New York: Macmillan, 1968), 15: 352-61.

13. William J. McGuire, "The Nature of Attitudes and Attitude Change," *Handbook of Social Psychology*, 2d ed. (Reading, Mass.: Addison-Wesley, 1968), 3: 139.

14. Meyer Schapiro, "Style," in *Aesthetics Today*, ed. Morris Philipson (Cleveland: World Publishing Co., 1961), p. 81.

15. Ibid., p. 82.

16. Derek J. De Solla Price, *Little Science, Big Science* (New York: Columbia University Press, 1963); Henry W. Menard, *Science: Growth and Change* (Cambridge: Harvard University Press, 1971); William D. Garvey and Belver C. Griffith, "Communication and Information Processing within Scientific Disciplines: Empirical Findings for Psychology," *Information Storage and Retrieval* 8 (1972) : 123-36.

17. Hagstrom, *Scientific Community*, p. 185, quoting a theoretical physicist: "In theoretical physics there are about five people who I would say are really first class. . . . The rest of theoretical physics is done by another 200 or 300 people around the world who essentially take the work of these five people and just work for a lifetime on it."

18. Cole and Cole, *Social Stratification in Science*, Ch. 4.

19. John Ziman, *Reliable Knowledge: An Exploration of the Grounds for Belief in Science* (Cambridge: Cambridge University Press, 1978), p. 130.

20. Ibid., p. 40. Cf. Menard, *Science*, p. 21: "Most scientific papers are ignored from the time the ink is dry."

21. Latour and Woolgar, *Laboratory Life*, p. 116.

22. Menard, *Science*, p. 143.

23. Walter J. Bate, "The Explosion of Knowledge: The Humanities," in *The Knowledge Explosion: Liberation and Limitation*, Centennial Colloquium at Boston College, ed. Francis Sweeney (New York: Farrar, Straus & Giroux, 1966), p. 108.

24. Hagstrom, *Scientific Community*, p. 229.

25. John Ziman, *Public Knowledge: The Social Dimension of Science* (Cambridge: Cambridge University Press, 1968), p. 123: "Experimental practitioners [*experienced practitioners* makes more sense] of any field of research will tell you what ideas are well understood, and accepted by everyone, and what is still speculative and uncertain, but there is a reluctance to set this down on paper." On the matter of consensus, see Michael Mulkay, "Consensus in Science," *Social Science Information* 17 (1978): 107-22.

26. Nevertheless, there are eminently respectable people who do exactly that, calling something knowledge though they realize it is not true. Machlup does (see note 1). Charles E. Lindblom and David K. Cohen, *Usable Knowledge: Social Science and Social Problem Solving* (New Haven: Yale University Press, 1979), p. 12, write that ordinary knowledge "is highly fallible, but we shall call it knowledge even if it is false. As in the case of scientific knowledge, whether it is true or false, knowledge is knowledge to anyone who takes it as a basis for some commitment or action." This simply means that they will call knowledge whatever an actor thinks he knows, even if in their opinion he is mistaken.

27. Michael Polanyi, "The Republic of Science: Its Political and Economic Theory," in *Criteria for Scientific Development: Public Policy and National Goals*, ed. Edward Shils (Cambridge: MIT Press, 1968), pp. 1-20. Donald T. Campbell, "Ethnocentrism of Disciplines and the Fish-Scale Model of Omniscience," in *Interdisciplinary Relationships in the Social Sciences*, ed. Muzafer Sherif and Carolyn W. Sherif (Chicago: Aldine,

1969), pp. 328-48, proposes an ideal of academic organization that exhibits Polanyi's overlapping competences but makes it clear that the actual situation is far from that ideal.

28. Stephen Cole, Jonathan R. Cole, and Gary A. Simon, "Chance and Consensus in Peer Review," *Science* 214 (1981): 885.

29. Alvin M. Weinberg, "Criteria for Scientific Choice," in Shils, *Criteria for Scientific Development*, pp. 21-33. On the question of allocation of support see the entire volume in which Weinberg's essay is reprinted and also Joseph Ben-David, "The Profession of Science and Its Powers," *Minerva* 10 (1972): 362-83, esp. pp. 376-83, and Brooks, *Government of Science*.

30. Eugene J. Meehan, "What Should Political Scientists Be Doing?" in *The Post-Behavioral Era: Perspectives on Political Science*, ed. George J. Graham, Jr., and George W. Carey (New York: David McKay, 1972), p. 67.

31. Michael Scriven, quoted in Irwin Silverman,"Why Social Psychology Fails," *Canadian Psychological Review* 18 (1977): 354.

32. Silverman, "Why Social Psychology Fails," p. 356. There is a voluminous literature on a crisis in social psychology; see, for example, Robert G. Boutilier, J. Christian Roed, and Ann C. Svendsen, "Crises in the Two Social Psychologies: A Critical Comparison," *Social Psychology Quarterly* 43 (1980): 5-17.

33. T. P. Waldron, "For the Want of a Theory," *TLS* ([London] *Times Literary Supplement*) 11 (July 1980): 785.

34. Boutilier, Roed, and Svendsen, "Crises in the Two Social Psychologies," mention others' defenses of their work in terms of publish-or-perish pressure, the desire to appear scientifically respectable, and the ability to complete a research program in reasonable time and cost. See Alvin Zander, "Psychology of Group Processes," *Annual Review of Psychology* 30 (1979), pp. 417-51, on why particular topics have been studied. He notes "the need among graduate students and other underfinanced investigators for inexpensive research results while using a method they are sure will be accepted by their peers" (p. 423).

35. See Lawrence Stone, "History and the Social Sciences in the Twentieth Century," in *The Future of History: Essays in the Vanderbilt University Centennial Symposium*, ed. Charles F. Delzell (Nashville, Tenn.: Vanderbilt University Press, 1977), pp. 3-41. One must not exaggerate the amount of work done in the new style, however; "at least 90 per cent of historical work published today is resolutely traditional in method, subject-matter and conceptualization," according to Geoffrey Barraclough, "History," in *Main Trends of Research in the Social and Human Sciences*, Pt. 2, vol. 1, *Anthropological and Historical Sciences, Aesthetics and*

the Sciences of Art, under the editorship of Jacques Havet (The Hague: Mouton, 1978), p. 435.

36. The mathematician Gordan on David Hilbert's new sort of mathematical proof: *Das ist nicht Mathematik. Das ist Theologie.* Constance Reid, *Hilbert* (New York: Springer-Verlag, 1970), p. 34. Jacques Barzun, *Clio and the Doctors: Psycho-history, Quanto-history and History,* (Chicago: University of Chicago Press, 1974), p. 24: "He knows as his eye ranges across a chart in all directions that he is not *reading history.*"

37. Jacob Viner, " 'Fashion' in Economic Thought," in *Report of the Sixth Conference of the Association of Princeton Graduate Alumni, 1957* (Princeton, 1957), p. 47.

38. Stephen Stich, "Desiring, Believing, and Doing," *TLS,* 27 June 1980, p. 737.

39. Michael Frisch, "American Urban History as an Example of Recent Historiography," *History and Theory* 18 (1979): 363.

40. Theodore J. Lowi, "The Politics of Higher Education," in *The Post-Behavioral Era,* p. 24.

41. Calvin S. Brown, "Faulkner, Criticism, and High Fashion," *Sewanee Review* 88 (1980): 636.

42. Edmund R. Leach, "Social Structure, I: The History of the Concept," *International Encyclopedia of the Social Sciences,* 14: 482.

43. Robert Crosman, "The Twilight of Critical Authority," *Annals of Scholarship* 1 (1980): 51.

44. Pitirim A. Sorokin, *Social and Cultural Dynamics* (New York: American Book Co., 1937), 2: 236.

45. Georg Simmel, "Fashion," *American Journal of Sociology* 62 (1957): 541-58.

46. Hagstrom, *Scientific Community,* pp. 177-84.

47. Kurt Lang and Gladys Lang, "Fashion: Identification and Differentiation in the Mass Society," in their *Collective Dynamics* (New York: Crowell, 1961), pp. 465-87; reprinted in *Dress, Adornment, and the Social Order,* ed. Mary Ellen Roach and Joanne Berbolz Eicher (New York: Wiley, 1965), pp. 322-46. The philosopher and historian R. G. Collingwood, discussing his claim that metaphysics is simply the study of changing "absolute presuppositions of thought," responds to the question whether such changes are merely changes of fashion by saying: "A 'change of fashion' is a superficial change, symptomatic perhaps of deeper and more important changes, but not itself deep or important." A change of "absolute presuppositions" is deep and important, "nor is there anything superficial or frivolous about it." So it cannot be a case of fashion. R. G. Collingwood, *An Essay on Metaphysics* (Oxford: Clarendon Press, 1940), p. 48.

48. Herbert Blumer, *International Encyclopedia of the Social Sciences*, s.v. "Fashion"; Herbert Blumer, "Fashion: From Class Differentiation to Collective Selection," *Sociological Quarterly* 10 (1969): 275-91.

49. Weinberg, "Criteria for Scientific Choice," p. 21: "The individual scientist must decide what science to do, what not to do: the totality of such judgments makes up his scientific taste." I would rather say it is a feature of his style and that his style reflects his taste.

50. Warren O. Hagstrom, "The Production of Culture in Science,"*American Behavioral Scientist* 19 (1976): 752-68. Cf. Diana Crane, *Invisible Colleges: Diffusion of Knowledge in Scientific Communities* (Chicago: University of Chicago Press, 1972), Ch. 2.

51. A. L. Kroeber, *Style and Civilizations* (Ithaca: Cornell University Press, 1957), p. 43.

52. Roy Lachman, Janet L. Lachman, and Earl C. Butterfield, *Cognitive Psychology and Information Processing: An Introduction* (Hillsdale, N.J.: Erlbaum, 1979), pp. 47-54.

53. Cf. Lang and Lang, "Fashion."

54. Gabriel Tarde, *The Laws of Imitation*, trans. Elsie Clews Parsons (New York: Holt, 1903), p. 140.

55. On fashion in scientific research, see especially Hagstrom, *Scientific Community*; Diana Crane, "Fashion in Science: Does it Exist?" *Social Problems* 16 (1969): 433-41; Honor B. Fell, "Fashion in Cell Biology," *Science* 132 (1960): 1625-27; Harold J. Morowitz, "Fashions in Science," *Science* 118 (1953): 331-32; Alvin M. Weinberg, *Reflections on Big Science* (Cambridge: MIT Press, 1968), esp. pp. 45-47; Fred Reif and Anselm Strauss, "The Impact of Rapid Discovery upon the Scientist's Career,"*Social Problems* 12 (1965): 297-311.

56. Thomas S. Kuhn, *The Essential Tension: Selected Studies in Scientific Tradition and Change* (Chicago: University of Chicago Press, 1977), p. 335. Given the widespread familiarity of Kuhn's *The Structure of Scientific Revolutions* (Chicago: University of Chicago Press, 1962, 2d ed., enlarged, 1970), it is natural to ask about the relation between his account of change and the present one. First, he is interested in the replacement of one theory by another; we are interested more generally in changes of styles of work. Next, Kuhn's famous paradigms are in a way mutually exclusive. It is characteristic of them that one replaces another completely; at any one time, only one paradigm reigns in a research area. But one fashion, one research style, need not drive out all other styles or fashions. Work may continue to be done in unfashionable styles, and there may be classic styles ("always in good taste") and other noncompeting styles (regional, national) that coexist with fashionable ones. Fashion can explain changes that do not represent the total victory

of a new paradigm. Further, it can explain small as well as large changes; most stylistic changes are not revolutionary. (It seems an advantage, not a disadvantage, to have an explanatory device that is applicable equally to large and small changes.) A Kuhnian revolution is a fundamental change in the way one sees the world; a change in fashion may make an older style of work seem not incorrect but simply boring, not mistaken but misdirected, not fruitless but frivolous. But finally, Kuhn says little about the process of gradual triumph of a new paradigm. He offers only what he terms an "impressionistic survey," noting that scientists accept the new for many reasons, including idiosyncrasies of autobiography and personality, even nationality or prior reputation of the innovator or teachers. He stresses that early adopters can do so only on faith. It appears that a Kuhnian revolution could be a case of fashion; Kuhn's story and ours are not in conflict.

57. P. B. Medawar and J. S. Medawar, *The Life Science: Current Ideas of Biology* (New York: Harper & Row, 1978), p. 96.

58. Lynn White, "New Horizons for the Social Sciences" in *Report of the Sixth Conference of the Association of Princeton Graduate Alumni*, p. 107.

59. Gerald D. Berreman, "Bringing It All Back Home: Malaise in Anthropology," in *Reinventing Anthropology*, ed. Dell Hymes (New York: Vintage Books, 1974), p. 83.

60. Stone, "History and the Social Sciences," pp. 6-7.

61. E. E. Kellett, *Fashion in Literature: A Study of Changing Taste* (London: Routledge, 1931), p. 64.

62. Imre Lakatos, "Falsification and the Methodology of Scientific Research Programmes," in *Criticism and the Growth of Knowledge*, ed. Imre Lakatos and Alan Musgrave (Cambridge: Cambridge University Press, 1970), p. 178. Lakatos was referring to Kuhn's view of scientific revolution, but he would surely have had the same reaction to the views being expressed here.

63. Blumer, "Fashion: From Class Differentiation to Collective Selection," p. 286.

64. For a refreshing review of the ideology and the actuality of scientific behavior, see Michael J. Mahoney, "Psychology of the Scientist: An Evaluative Review," *Social Studies of Science*, 9 (1979): 349-75.

65. J. O. Wisdom, "The Nature of 'Normal' Science," in *The Philosophy of Karl Popper*, ed. Paul Arthur Schillp (LaSalle, Ill.: Open Court, 1974), 2: 832.

66. Crane notes that it is hard to discover motives for scientific work, hence hard to decide whether fashion is present in any particular instance, and so limits her own discussion of fashion to purely external questions of what can be counted—telling us, consequently, nothing about fashion. Crane, "Fashion in Science," pp. 433-41.

67. Jorgen Rasmussen, " 'Once You've Made a Revolution, Everything's the Same': Comparative Politics," in *The Post-Behavioral Era*, p. 79.

68. Lee Sigelman, "How to Succeed in Political Science by Being Very Trying: A Methodological Sampler," PS (*Political Science*) 10 (1977): 302.

69. Stow Persons, "The Wingspread Papers," *Reviews in American History* (December 1979): 447.

70. Maurice B. Line and A. Sandison, " 'Obsolescence'and Changes in the Use of Literature with Time," *Journal of Documentation* 30 (1974): 283-350.

71. E. Rosenfeld, quoted in Harold Orlans, *Contracting for Knowledge* (San Francisco: Jossey-Bass, 1973), p. 189.

4 THE KNOWLEDGE INDUSTRY: INSTITUTIONAL AUTHORITY

Institutional Authority

It is not only individuals in whom we recognize cognitive authority; we recognize it as well in books, instruments, organizations, and institutions. Many believe that religious texts are infallible revelations from the supernatural and infallible sources of historical knowledge and moral guidance. Reference books in large numbers are granted cognitive authority, which is not simply the authority of their compilers transferred to the book, for we may not know or much care who the compilers were. For many people "the dictionary" (as if there were only one) has absolute cognitive authority; questions of orthography, pronunciation, and meaning are considered closed when the dictionary has been consulted. A newspaper, a magazine, or a television program can have cognitive authority independent of the particular individuals (who may be anonymous) who produce the publication. For very naive people, any publication may carry authority; the mere fact of something being said in print or over a broadcast medium is enough to give it weight. Instruments have authority. Reference to a clock, thermometer, or barometer may settle questions or give great weight to an opinion. Organizations—churches, governments, political parties—may have cognitive authority independent of the particular individuals occupying their offices. The point of a formal organization is to give authority to offices that does not depend exclusively on the characteristics of the individuals who fill them. This is obvious for administrative authority but holds as well for cognitive authority. A particular occupant of an office may, by blatant malperformance, be blamed not only for individual misconduct but for bringing the office into disrepute, hence weakening its cognitive authority.

The prime example of institutionalized cognitive authority is the pope speaking ex cathedra. The voice is not simply that of a particular person but of a corporation sole, a one-person corporate body. The word of the central committee of a political party is not taken as the word of those few people who happen to be members of it at a particular time. It may be the voice of the party itself and carry massive weight for party members. Insofar as we think that a specialized occupational group possesses a body of art or craft that is the common possession of the whole group, we may recognize cognitive authority as residing in the group as a collective entity, a corporate body. So we may feel that although individual members of the medical profession may be incompetent, dishonest, and downright dangerous to health, the profession itself is basically competent.

In our time, the prime locus of institutional cognitive authority is the scientific community, the social institution of science. What this institution includes and what it excludes are matters of controversy. It certainly encompasses physics, chemistry, and biology, the basic natural sciences. It also includes the formal sciences: mathematics, logic, statistics. It includes earth and space sciences and applied biomedical, engineering, and agricultural sciences. (The distinction between basic and applied sciences is difficult to make in practice but will not concern us, nor will the precise location of the boundary between science and technology.) Whether the social and behavioral sciences are branches of science is an open question, as is the question whether subjects like history are parts of the humanities or of the social sciences. The question of what science includes is one local to the English-speaking world; elsewhere words corresponding to science are used to cover all branches of systematic organized inquiry.[1] The humanities are not branches of science, but they are certainly branches of *Wissenschaft*. But it can be argued that here the idiosyncrasies of the English language in fact reflect a real distinction that is blurred elsewhere: one between studies that have and those that lack institutional authority. The question whether a study is, or should be recognized as, a branch of science is the question whether it has, or should be recognized as having, the kind and degree of institutional authority that the recognized natural and formal sciences have.

The Authority of the Sciences

It is safe to say that most college-educated people in our society undoubtedly recognize the cognitive authority of science as an institution; it is not safe to say much more than this. Our information about what people in general think comes from a few questions asked of a few people in public opinion polls and otherwise from scattered and unsystematic observations and impressions. For instance, in California in 1981 nearly half of those queried in an opinion poll said that they had "a lot of confidence" in "research scientists," and most of the rest claimed to have "some confidence." Only a few claimed "not much confidence." The "research scientists" stood at the top of the list, followed by the local police department, universities and colleges, and the president of the United States.[2] This suggests recognition of the cognitive authority of science but tells us little about what people think is its sphere of authority or its degree of authority. Do people think that science as an institution settles the questions with which it deals? Is it not only authoritative but the exclusive authority for questions within its sphere? And what is its sphere? We cannot expect that many people have decided views on such questions because the questions do not arise in daily life for most of us. Given what is known about the amount of formal education in science that is received in secondary schools and colleges, one must suspect that popular ideas of science are vague, shallow, and inconsistent. A vague sentiment that research scientists are credible is quite consistent with a readiness to give equal respect to the claims of astrology and the occult as coequal sources of knowledge. And confidence in science in some spheres is compatible with belief in the inerrancy of the Bible.

If we want a better idea of the institutional authority of science than is provided by public opinion polls, we may resort to an imaginary device: a thought experiment. We may imagine the deliberations of a jury chosen randomly from the population (excluding children and the mentally handicapped). Juries have to decide how much weight to give to the testimony of individual witnesses. We can try to imagine a jury empaneled to decide how much weight should be given to testimony from various groups of witnesses: natural scientists, social scientists, historians, theologians, and so on. Spokesmen for each group would present claims for cognitive authority and defend their claims by ducing considerations analogous to those described in chapter 2; spokesmen for other groups would attempt to rebut those claims and put forward their own. The jury's decision after discussion and reflection may not correspond to the prior beliefs or opinions of any individual juror, for the process may create opinions where none existed before, as well as change those that did exist. In addition, a collective decision may please no one in the collectivity. Yet it will reflect the considered opinions of the jurors and, with luck, may represent considered public opinion. It is not hard to imagine such a jury and such a task. The difficulty is that it is too easy and too likely to produce different results at different times and for different individuals. But let us try it just the same. What will be the claims for authority on the part of the representatives of science, what their justifications, and what the results?

The sciences claim exclusive jurisdiction over questions within their spheres of inquiry. It is argued that the chief distinction of the natural sciences is to tell us about things outside the range of ordinary experience: entities much too small to be visible to the naked eye or too large to be taken in by a glance; things far away in space and in time; processes that are too rapid, or too slow, to be detected by our unaided senses. Their instrumentation allows them to do this. Unless we accept their stories, we have no way of finding out about the things they describe. Science also employs special conceptual tools, mathematics being the most obvious example. But it has no special tricks of thinking, argument, proof, or reasoning; its methods of thought are simply refinements of common sense.[3] Its real claim to authority rests on the fact that it investigates what others do not, or cannot successfully.

So far the case is not made, for scientists might be experts without authority, exploring without success an area that others ignore. The case continues with the scientist pointing to two features: scientific predictions that can be verified by others and applications of science in technology. Science claims, and technology agrees, that much of modern technology rests on the application of scientific findings; and the jury can decide whether the technology exists and works. Demonstrations of predictive ability can be arranged for the jury as it wishes.

Still the case is not made. Individual predictive successes and discoveries with clear practical applications do not automatically lead to justification of institutional authority. Granting that Newton, Einstein, and Mendeleev were experts is one thing; granting that science as an institution should have cognitive authority is another. For this, science points to its internal consensus. Like every other group of inquirers, science aims at results on which all competent inquirers will agree; unlike most other groups, it achieves this goal to a surprising degree.[4] Scientific textbooks and reference books contain accounts of what is accepted by the whole scientific community and what has been collectively agreed on—there is a lot of it. Science does not lack disagreements, however. There are plenty of current controversies, which may or may not end in the universal triumph of a single story. But science often settles its disagreements and comes to a single generally accepted doctrine. Now unanimity of opinion is essential for institutional authority.[5] A group might consist of a dozen people, each recognized as a cognitive authority. The group deserves to be recognized in this way as a group only to the extent to which it speaks with one voice. If the institution has no agreed view on a particular question, then the weight of the institution cannot attach to any particular view. But if there is an agreed view, that is consequently the view of the institution, at least for the time being. And the claim for institutional authority for science rests finally on the fact that there are a great many views that can be represented correctly as those of the institution. It can be said impersonally that "science tells us . . ." or "chemistry shows that. . . ." Science has a territory in which it is without serious competition, it can show strong predictive and technological indications of competence, and it shows, over a wide range, a common front.

Such might be the case for the natural sciences. A different sort of case would be made for the formal sciences, which we will pass by. The jury might be surprised that no claim is made for the existence of a special method, the scientific method, but on that there is no consensus. The jury might also be somewhat confused at finding technology distinguished from science and offered as only indirect evidence of science's competence, for the jurors probably start by supposing that science and technology are the same.[6] The jury listens not only to the case for science but to rebuttals by representatives of revealed religion and the occult. After deliberation, it decides that science as an institution deserves cognitive authority but not absolute authority since, as the science representatives admit, today's scientific consensus differs from yesterday's and probably from tomorrow's. Hence today's claims, even if they are unanimous, should be met with some skepticism, though they may serve as the best working assumptions for practical purposes where they are relevant. The claim of exclusive jurisdiction is granted where unopposed; where opposed, as in questions of ultimate origin and ultimate destiny, it is not granted. The jury recognizes that on such questions, scientific opinion is relevant but not decisive.

Nothing is claimed for this imaginary jury decision except that it is a not unlikely outcome of an actual trial of the imagined sort. A similar outcome might be expected for the case of the formal sciences, though in that case it is more likely that the jury would be prepared to grant not only exclusive jurisdiction but also absolute authority. In their sphere, the mathematicians would be recognized as facing no competition at all from other groups, and others would be prepared to take their unanimous verdicts as conclusively settling questions. The outcomes of such trials will certainly differ, depending on whether we require unanimity or something less than unanimity for a decision. Although it is hard to imagine a jury in which anyone denied all authority to science, it is easy to imagine one in which some members denied it exclusive jurisdiction over any sphere, being prepared to recognize a wide variety of nonscientific sources as sharing authority with science (for instance, astrologers or clairvoyants). The most we should expect is that a majority will agree that scientific opinion has no serious competition within a large part of the sphere to which it lays claim; if scientists cannot settle the questions within their area, no other group can either. Note that we have said nothing to suggest that this imaginary decision is one that a jury ought to arrive at, or that a perfectly informed jury would arrive at.

We take the fact that a person has successfully gone through a systematic course of scientific training as evidence of his expert standing and his qualification to be recognized as having cognitive authority because we recognize the cognitive authority of the institution that stands behind his claims. An accredited member of a competent community is presumed competent until proven otherwise. As with any other sort of claim to authority, indications of corruption, dishonesty, fraud, mental incapacity, and the like can lead to rejection of the claim. But the initial presumption is of a basic level of competence in some area of science. Since the accrediting process does not work perfectly, this presumption may lead to disappointment. Frequent and serious disappointments would call the accrediting process and ultimately the authority of the institution into question. Evidence of venality, concealment or distortion of information for personal gain, or of political or ideological bias destroys the credibility of individual scientists and, if found on a large scale, of the institution itself. Perhaps most people who examined the matter would now agree that such evidence has not much threatened scientific authority. It may not always be so.

A group of specialists may agree among themselves on the current answer to some question within their range of interest, and consider the question to be closed. In their view, they have gained or produced some knowledge. If others grant them exclusive jurisdiction over the question and recognize them as having the ability to settle questions within their jurisdiction, they will be prepared to take the group consensus as practically settling the matter, at least for the present. They will thus recognize the group as knowledge producers. If, however, others deny them exclusive jurisdiction or refuse to recognize their ability to settle questions within their sphere of interest, then they will be recognized only as producers of opinion, which may indeed carry weight but not enough to settle questions for the outsiders. Since different people may have very different views on these matters, the question whether a specialist group produces knowledge may be open. If practically everyone agrees about jurisdiction and competence, the question is socially closed:

the group is generally recognized as a knowledge producer or not, as the case may be. So whether one makes a contribution to knowledge depends not only on what one does but what others think of the group within which one works.

When a new specialist group arises and begins production, commonly it looks for recognition of its claims to jurisdiction and competence from other already established specialties, for if they recognize its claims, others who recognize the authority of those specialties will be likely to recognize the newcomer's claims.[7] Failing to get such recognition or perhaps rejecting established authority, the new group might appeal directly to the general populace, promising startling and visible achievements. It might attract a following despite the skepticism or hostility of the already entrenched specialties. In such a case, the matter of their ability to produce knowledge would be socially open, perhaps finally to be closed either by general acceptance or by their disappearance. So we see the complexity of the apparently simple question, "Does this group produce knowledge?" The question cannot be answered as one might answer the question, "Does this factory actually produce any bicycles?" by simply looking at the products. But it has to be borne in mind that the question can be approached in two different ways. For the outside observer (perhaps from another culture), it is answered by investigating whether the group's claims are in fact taken as settling questions. For the insider trying to decide whether the group deserves to be recognized as having cognitive authority within its sphere, it is not a question of whether others do but of whether one should take them as having the ability to settle questions.

The Social Sciences

The situation is very different with the social and behavioral sciences: economics, sociology, anthropology, political science, and psychology. Officially these are recognized as branches of science; they are included in the list of scientific specializations used for the National Register of Scientific and Technical Personnel kept by the National Science Foundation, and they are represented by separate sections in the National Academy of

Sciences, the organization that since 1863 has been the official scientific adviser to the U. S. government.[8] But as an institution or a group of distinct institutions, the social sciences present a strikingly different picture from the other sciences. They do not investigate phenomena beyond the range of ordinary experience; they do not present large bodies of agreed results; they cannot offer their predictive abilities or the successful practical application of their findings as indirect evidence of their competence as institutions. Their claim to exclusive jurisdiction and to institutional authority is weak.

It is even harder to get an idea of what the public thinks of social science as an institution than to get an idea of its opinion of natural science; even the thin evidence of public opinion polls is lacking on this point. But scattered and impressionistic evidence is plentiful, and imaginary proceedings before a jury are easy to construct. No jury will recognize the social sciences' exclusive jurisdiction over the areas of human life that they study. All of us are somewhat knowledgeable about the subject matter of the social sciences: ordinary life. Social scientists investigate the same sorts of phenomena as do journalists, social critics and commentators, businessmen, government officials, and novelists. The business of the social sciences is everybody's business and not left by default to academic social scientists to investigate. No one will agree that political questions are the exclusive preserve of political scientists. Businessmen will not concede that economists' views on the economy are always to be given greater weight than their own views. Who will grant that we ought to get our views of social relations from sociologists? Any claim of exclusive jurisdiction would be laughed out of court.

The case for a grant of institutional cognitive authority of a high degree would have to consist of showing special competence, an ability to gain knowledge and understanding by means not available to others, that entitles the social sciences either to special deference on questions that fall within the scope of ordinary observation, experience, and reflection, or to authority on questions concerning what is inaccessible to ordinary observation and experience. And the claim for institutional authority might rest on a claim that the social sciences are particularly competent at the construction or discovery of theories that allow explanation and prediction of social phenomena. Let us confine ourselves for now to this particular claim: that the social sciences should be recognized as authoritative sources of social theory.

The difficulty for the case is that by their own accounts, the social sciences appear to have been unsuccessful at the task of constructing social theories. One prominent social scientist writes that "the major value of modern social science is . . . to promote scepticism about bad social theories," and another says that "the single most important discovery of social science in these last decades is that social science does not yield the kind of knowledge of society—and the kind of power over society—that natural science possesses vis-à-vis the natural world."[9] For most of this century, leaders in the social sciences have deliberately sought to imitate the aims and methods of the natural sciences, looking for laws to allow explanation and prediction in the social world as the laws of physics and chemistry do in the physical world. They have found none. "No one believes that this kind of theory [of the sort found in the natural sciences] exists at the moment in sociology or that it is likely to develop in the near future."[10] The best that can be done is to produce limited generalizations about central tendencies, with low explanatory power.[11]

Economics is the social science that has had greatest worldly success, and economics appears to have powerful and rigorous theories and analytic techniques. But even economists do not agree that the theories describe the world. For many, they seem rather to be "helpless in the face of reality," however elaborate and internally self-consistent.[12] Outside economics there is little semblance of unanimity on any social theory. And even inside economics, one can claim substantial unanimity only by denying that dissenters (such as Marxian and radical economists) are really economists at all.

Factionalism and poverty of agreed results show in textbooks and reference works. Instead of standardized textbook presentations of generally accepted theories and laws, social science textbooks put forth what a historian of science harshly describes as "intuitive generalities dressed up as empirical laws, and insecure theoretical speculations masquerading as fundamental explanations."[13] Instead of standard reference works full of precise numerical detail on physical constants like the Gmelin *Hand-*

buch der anorganischen Chemie, one finds the discursive *International Encyclopedia of the Social Sciences* or the vague banalities of Berelson and Steiner's *Human Behavior: An Inventory of Findings*.[14] The requirement that social science show special competence at investigating ordinary matters or else reveal hitherto undiscovered or inaccessible features of ordinary life is not satisfied by findings such as: "In a modern democratic industrial country, with substantial social heterogeneity, political parties must appeal to a range of social groups in order to secure a majority."[15]

What makes a science, says George Homans, is not its results but its aims. Because the social sciences aim at establishing "more or less general relationships between properties of nature," they are thus sciences.[16] A grant of institutional cognitive authority requires more than good intentions; it requires reasons for thinking that the good intentions are coupled with competence. The lack of general agreement on social theories of any more than commonsense plausibility and generality spoils the claim for institutional authority. Writing a hundred years ago, George Cornewall Lewis noted that "in the moral and political sciences, there is a less general consensus than in the physical . . . hence, the writers on political economy who have arrived at true conclusions do not carry the authority which is due to them because those conclusions are disputed by other scientific writers."[17] Lewis thought he knew who those were who had arrived at true conclusions. If one does not think one knows that, the problem is to decide which, if any, deserve authority. If they were in agreement, it would still be a problem to decide whether their agreed views deserved to be taken seriously, whether the institutional view was a weighty one. But where they are all in disagreement, there is no question of institutional authority.

As to the ability to predict, it is unlikely that many social scientists would now claim that their special competence is indirectly shown by their predictive capacity; it is more likely that they would argue that failures of prediction should not be taken as proof of incapacity.[18] Nor can the social sciences claim much authority on the basis of the successful application of their social theories, as science gains indirect credit from the success of its technological applications.[19]

There are indeed useful and successful activities such as large-scale data collection in censuses and public opinion polls that might be termed applied social science, but it is not clear that they actually apply anything in the way of general theory previously developed in pure social science. Statistics, not social theory, is being applied. Other fields of social technology seem at best weak evidence of practical application of social theory. The field of education does not provide strikingly successful accomplishments reported to rest on application of social or psychological theories. Nor do the fields of criminology or social welfare. The field of administration—in business, government, and nonprofit organizations—only doubtfully provides evidence of strong theoretical underpinnings on which practical success depends. Psychiatry's status as a branch of technology is subject to fierce debate, but it does not function as a technological demonstration of the power of psychological theory.[20] In general, where physical technology is a powerful index of the competence of science to the outside observer, social technology to him seems a weak index or no index of the competence of the social sciences as makers of social theory. This is admitted by some social scientists: "If we removed all knowledge of scientific psychology from our world, problems in interpersonal relations might easily be coped with and solved much as before."[21] Explaining the disappointing results of applied social science, one psychologist notes that "only when you know something can you apply it, and, because the discipline is so new, too little knowledge has been accumulated in most areas to enable social scientists to do productive applied research . . . there is no clear framework on which to base applied research, no coherent body of knowledge from which to derive hypotheses or make predictions."[22]

The case for the cognitive authority of the social sciences would be strengthened if it were supported by an institution already recognized as having authority. The situation would be analogous to the personal recommendation principle discussed in chapter 2. If science says that one can trust the social sciences, and if we trust science, then we would be likely to think it proper to trust the social sciences. Unfortunately for the social sciences, such endorsement is unlikely. If anything is likely to be agreed on among scientists, it is that the record of social science in producing "theories that have scope and coherence, that grow—

and that throw off predictions of unexpected new facts" is thin, that they are "immature and ineffective fields of inquiry."[23] Such testimony would further weaken the case for cognitive authority. The case for institutional cognitive authority for the social sciences is likely to be decided by the jury against the social sciences. Since that case centered on the claim of special competence in the area of social theory, this does not settle the matter, for claims to authority might be based on other kinds of competence. So far, it appears that recognition of the expertise and authority of particular individuals will not rest on the evidence provided by institutional accreditation. If the institution lacks authority, it cannot pass it on to individuals by accredited courses of systematic study. Whatever authority the individual acquires will be a matter of evaluation of the individual claim on its own merits, and credentials will lack the force they carry in the formal and natural sciences.

Two points deserve further comment. If factionalism ruins claims to institutional authority, it does not do the same to factional authority. Marxist and neoclassical economists and their followers may be unperturbed by the others' existence; so might followers of Skinner and of Freud. Each faction might indeed speak with a single voice, so that one could speak of *the* Marxist view on a certain matter, *the* neoclassical line, and so on. That a jury reflecting public opinion in general will not find sufficient reason to recognize any of the factions as having cognitive authority does not mean that there will not be large groups of people who do recognize the authority of particular factions. And for a follower of a particular faction, appropriate accreditation may be evidence of both expertise and right to cognitive authority. But for others, the social sciences will be the best place to find the phenomenon of the expert without authority or, better, the doctrinal quasi-expert: the person deeply learned in the doctrines of a particular school or faction, a great expert in Freudian psychoanalytic doctrine or neoclassical economic theory, but not recognized as a great authority, or any authority at all, on human behavior or the explanation of actual economic phenomena.

The position of psychology in the array of social and behavioral sciences is somewhat anomalous. Parts of psychology are probably best counted as branches of biology, studying physical rather than mental processes. Within the clearly nonbiological part of psychology, behaviorism for a long time dominated theoretical inquiry and psychology tried to confine itself to what is publicly observable. It appears that psychologists increasingly are prepared to attempt the study of unconscious mental operations and so claim a subject matter that does indeed lie outside the range of ordinary observation (or that will be admitted to do so by those who agree that the workings of the mind are not open to simple introspection).[24] So far, however, external evidence of special competence at exploring and gaining knowledge about this special subject matter appears to be wanting.

History

For knowledge of the past, we turn to historians. If we suppose we are turning toward a well-defined social institution, however, we are mistaken. Historians are dispersed and loosely organized. In fact, large numbers of them count themselves as natural scientists first and historians second, if at all. Cosmologists, the historians of the universe; geologists, historians (among other things) of the earth; paleontologists, historians of life: these are scientists but also historians. *Natural history* would be a good term for such studies, but it has the wrong connotations. Each branch of human culture has its complement of historians: of music, art, literature; of science, technology, agriculture, medicine, business, education, war; of religion, philosophy, politics, economic life, economic doctrine, social life, social doctrine. Each profession, each occupation, each sport, is a subject for a historian. Every sort of artifact and process can have its own historians. There are histories of postage stamps and of houses, of sword making, of book binding, of music printing, of piano playing, and so on. Biographers are historians.[25] Organizations have histories and people to write them. There are historians of language and of place names. Everyone who writes an autobiography or book of memoirs is "his own historian."[26] The number of people who write history is very large.

If biographers are considered as writing history, they are not admitted to be historians by people who teach in college history departments. For that matter, "it is not usual to regard historians of literature, of science, of painting, or of philosophy as 'historians' "; the term *historian* is claimed by, if not invariably limited to, practitioners of general history rather than special history.[27] Members of the various special branches of science think of themselves as scientists and recognize members of the other branches as scientists; members of the large group of people who write histories apparently do not all think of themselves as historians or recognize the others as historians. If history is a distinct social institution at all, it is a very much less clearly organized one than is science, and membership in it is much less clearly defined than membership in the institution of science. But let us suppose that it nevertheless exists and might claim cognitive authority on the grounds of special competence at describing and explaining the past. What kind of case might be made to our imaginary jury?

Since historians generally avoid prediction and do not seem to be particularly successful when they do try it, that test would be unavailable to the outsider. Nor are there technological applications to use as indirect tests of special competence, so we must look for other signs. Consensus on findings would be persuasive, but consensus apparently is not expected within the ranks of historians. The author of one of the most famous historical works of modern times, Jacob Burckhardt, begins by saying that "the same studies which have served for this work might easily, in other hands, not only receive a wholly different treatment and application, but lead also to essentially different conclusions."[28] If that is indeed the situation not just for the particular case of Renaissance history but for history in general, then the situation is that one cannot say "history says that . . ." but only "this historian says so and so, but that historian says, in opposition, such and such." And why are we outsiders to believe that historians have a special competence at describing and explaining the past, if applications of that presumed competence lead to inconsistent results, if even a historian will say that "whereas there is one natural science, there are many histories, overlapping and contradictory, argumentative and detached, biased and ambiguous"?[29]

There may be other telling signs of special competence—for

instance, signs of an arcane technique or method for extracting conclusions from bits of evidence, but such evidence is hard to find. Works on historical method are easily accessible to the layman and contain no procedural instructions for getting conclusions out of data that go beyond what is evident to common sense.[30] One historian has flatly denied that history has any methods: "Method for the historian is only a metaphor to say that he is rational and resourceful, imaginative and conscientious."[31] Historians do not appear to have special ways of explaining past actions and events; they seem to appeal to commonsense truisms.[32] Their accounts of human behavior mostly depend on everyday notions of the motivations for action and inaction; when they do not, they draw on highly controversial theories from psychology and the social sciences to produce sharply contested kinds of work (as in psychohistory).[33] History does not appear to have or claim to have any special body of theory of its own for use in explanation; insofar as it borrows from the social sciences, it borrows failed or unsubstantiated theories.

It appears there is no strong case to be made for recognition of the cognitive authority of history as an institution, and not clear that there even is an institution. The authority of individual historians will rest on evidence of study and experience, inside or outside an academic environment; and when it comes to choice among conflicting experts, the outsider will have to rely on the advice of those he trusts or on the final test of intrinsic plausibility.

Social Science as Current History

The attempt of the social sciences to make themselves theoretical sciences on the pattern of physics, chemistry, or experimental biology has been a failure, but that does not mean that they have accomplished nothing. Not all of science is theoretical or experimental; much of astronomy, geology, oceanography, paleontology, and ecology is purely descriptive of present and past conditions, and none the worse for that. If we oppose natural history to human history and look at the actual content of the masses of books and journals reporting the results of social science research, it is easy to see the appropriateness of counting the bulk of social science research into the category of work on human history. Only an unnecessarily narrow view of history would lead us to exclude descriptions of the recent past from the category of historical writing while including descriptions of the more remote past. Why think that history starts fifty or a hundred years ago? By the time a description of what happens today is written, it will be a description of things past; by the time the political scientist writes an account of a campaign or a public opinion survey, the situation described is well past. He has the advantage over the more ancient historian that he gathered his materials himself, while the ancient historian has to depend on materials others gathered. But presumably the ancient historian would be happy to assemble his own materials if a time machine could be developed to transport him back to ancient Greece or colonial America and make history an observational study.

Much of social science consists of descriptions of situations and conditions rather than of sequences of events; and if we think that history has to be essentially a description of sequences of events connected to make a story, as some historians indeed still do, then we would have to distinguish historiography, ways of writing history, from sociography, ways of describing society at a time or over a period of time. But historians themselves increasingly use nonnarrative forms of writing; they see themselves as practicing social science on the past, using the techniques and procedures of social scientists insofar as the state of the available evidence allows. They practice demography, econometrics, and sociology on the past. History has even been described, by a historian, as "retrospective cultural anthropology."[34] But if history, as the study of the relatively long-past past, can be considered as retrospective social science, obviously social science can equally well be described as current history, the practice of history on the near past and the present, which is constantly turning into past.

Historians are more likely to say that history has become one of the social sciences than to say that it is becoming clear that the social sciences are branches of history. But the latter view is more fruitful and illuminating, since grouping them all under the heading of social science is likely to give undue prominence to the abortive quest for general laws, while grouping them all under the heading of history is likely to give proper prominence to the element of sheer description. An enormous amount of work in sociology, political science, anthropology, and economics is simply descriptive and interpretive of more or less recent conditions. Ethnographies, surveys of political opinions and studies of voting behavior, collections of economic statistics, social surveys: all describe social life, whether or not they narrate particular incidents or tell connected stories of events as traditional histories did. Much of the social data collected with the aim of discovering or validating claims about invariant laws of individual and social behavior are best now taken as simply descriptions of temporary conditions in particular groups of people.[35] What aims and pretends to be more than simply description and interpretation of local temporary conditions is probably only of value as current history. If we classify the social sciences on the basis of their accomplishments rather than their ambitions, we will group them as branches of recent or current history.

In recent times, increasing numbers of social scientists appear to have turned away from the idea that social science should imitate natural science and moved toward (or back to) the belief that their task is the description and interpretation of social life, even to the admission that they practice an art form. Those who have done so might be amenable to having their work classified as a branch of a large study of history, whose other practitioners have long been ready to recognize the degree to which their works are works of art.[36]

History and Authority

The social sciences might make a claim for cognitive authority based not on a special competence at the construction of social theory but on other grounds: a special competence at social description and interpretation. The claim would be that although social scientists engage in the same sort of descriptive and interpretative activity as do journalists and other social observers, they do it better, by virtue of special training at social observation and analysis. This is the same sort of claim that professional historians might make: amateurs can indeed do it, but professionals do it better by virtue of their special training at discovering, reading, evaluating, and interpreting historical records.

How is the layman, or our imaginary jury of laymen, to evaluate such claims? Someone must decide whether particular pieces of current description or past description are better than others. If the decision is left to the professionals, it is clear how the decision will go. The jury cannot be expected to turn themselves into historians or social scientists to determine for themselves, by independent research, the relative worth of samples of description. Adopting professional standards would prejudice the case anyway; the question is about the value of professional standards. As in the case of past history, we could look for indications that professionals have arcane techniques that they employ in observation and analysis. But those techniques might not seem extraordinary: asking people questions and tabulating their answers, spending time in a community sharing the activities of the group, reading newspapers, books, parliamentary debates and the like. These ways of collecting data do not look different from quite ordinary ways of finding out things, though if people spend a great deal of time employing them, it is evident that they can collect more data than one normally can. Statistical analysis of data can indeed look complex to the layman, though very simple statistical analysis is familiar enough in ordinary life. But given the evidence (which would be readily forthcoming) that methods of statistical analysis can be chosen in various ways and with quite different results, almost at the pleasure of the analyst, a jury might find that it was simply not convinced that arcane data analysis was invariably preferable to simpler, or even nonstatistical analysis. The upshot might then be that the claim that professional description is generally better than nonprofessional description because it is based on superior trained ability at description and analysis was simply not proved.

This conclusion is consistent with a recent evaluation of social science research by Lindblom and Cohen. Social science, they claim, cannot achieve scientifically definitive or conclusive answers on questions of interest to policymakers; social scientists cannot settle the questions they raise, even for the scientific community.[37] Even if they could, they might not be authoritative for others; others would not take their word as settling the question. Social science cannot hope to be independently authoritative or, in our terms, absolutely authoritative for others. It can hope to be dependently authoritative if its results confirm what is already known on other grounds, by ordinary knowledge, the result of unprofessional common sense, casual empiricism, or thoughtful speculation and analysis.[38] But that in effect means that a piece of information or opinion is given no special weight on the ground that it comes from a social scientist. One is glad to have them confirm what one already knows but does not give great weight to what they say if it contradicts what one already believes. No cognitive authority there, unless one has other grounds for granting it to a particular individual.

If neither historians as conventionally understood nor historians in our wider sense can claim institutional authority over the whole sphere in which they operate, still it is likely to be allowed that the more closely they stick to the description of things that might in principle have been directly observed, and the less they do in the way of explanation or interpretation, the safer it is to trust them. When they report what they have in fact observed, they are entitled to the same credence one would give to any ordinarily competent observer presumed to be trustworthy. When they reconstruct past events and conditions of the simple sort that might have been witnessed, then so far as they proceed on commonsense principles of inference and evidence, we may be happy to assume that they are as capable as we would have been. We may be prepared to allow that history does deliver to us a mass of more or less elementary factual information that we can comfortably assume to be established beyond reasonable doubt, along with constructions put on these facts that we cannot so comfortably assume to be established at all.

Geisteswissenschaften and Soft Classification

The conclusion that the social sciences and history lack the institutional authority of the formal and natural sciences does not necessarily require an attempt to explain why this should be so, but it inevitably invites one. It is a serious matter that we seem unable to get, from the most careful professional inquiry, the sort of knowledge about human affairs that we seem to be able to get about the natural world and the abstract worlds of the formal sciences. It is not that we lack knowledge about human affairs but that we seem unable, by professional inquiry, to improve much on what we can learn by ordinary experience, observation, and reflection. Why should this be so? If what we have to say about history and the social sciences is correct, then it applies to anything we now try to say about why they are so relatively weak at explanation. This explanation can expect to be given no greater weight than other attempts to explain the human situation. With that understood, let us anyway see what we can say.

The failure of the social sciences to attain the kind of generally accepted and predictively successful theories found in the natural sciences is not simply a failure of intellect or of effort.[39] Nor is it a simple organizational failure that might be repaired by rejuggling academic boundaries, encouraging interdisciplinary studies, or engaging natural scientists to instruct social scientists on proper techniques. And it is not a question of time, a matter of youth having to wait for maturity. Works of history and social science written in ancient Greece are still worth reading. The explanation lies in the subject matter, in the difference made by the fact that humans have minds full of ideas and dreams that influence their actions, and by the fact that they interact with each other not simply as physical systems but as partners in joint understandings and misunderstandings and in competition and conflict. It lies in the fact that people's activities depend not only on what they want and what they think they are able to do but also on what they think is right and wrong, permissible and impermissible. And it lies in the fact that their ways of behavior are subject to change: deliberate, forced, responsive to changes of taste and mood. We cannot expect that the study of social processes will give the same kind of result as does the study of physical processes. Things change drastically when one moves from studying matter in motion to studying behavior dependent on and responsive to information and imagination.

Bringing human history and the social sciences together in a single large category, labeled history, but meaning human history of near and remote past, accounts to recognition of what in German is called the *Geisteswissenschaften* as a special category of studies. For well over a century it has been argued, and denied with counterarguments, that the human studies, the phrase we might use to translate *Geisteswissenschaften*, are and must be different both in aims and in methods from the *Naturwissenschaften*, the natural sciences.[40] As to aims, the most familiar way of putting it is that the natural sciences are nomothetic; they aim to find laws governing repeatable phenomena. The human studies are ideographic; they try to grasp the unique features of unrepeatable phenomena. This distinction is unsatisfactory since the natural sciences include large descriptive branches, and the human studies have tried to find laws or at least rough generalizations governing repeatable phenomena. As to method, it has been claimed that the human studies, unlike the natural sciences, do and must employ a special method of *Verstehen* or understanding, which means grasping the meaning, significance, intention, or purpose of human actions, a method without counterpart in the natural sciences, where intentionality is either absent in the phenomena under study or can be ignored, as in the study of human beings as simply physical systems. The human studies are held to be interpretive or hermeneutic studies, as the natural sciences are not. But there is another way of approaching the matter by looking not at the aim or the methods of inquiry but at the character of the things of interest to the human studies: the nature of the objects and their characteristics.

It is common to contrast the hard physical sciences with the soft social sciences, having in mind that the physical sciences often attain exact and definite results of great generality: precise numerical values for physical constants, theories relating measurable variables in universally valid and definite relationships. The social sciences, on the other hand, arrive only at vague approximations to general laws. But it is rewarding to consider the distinction between hard and soft as applying to the kinds of things studied in the different sciences. When we turn from the natural world to the world of human thought and action, we turn from a world of more or less natural units to one of arbitrary, unstable, or amorphous units. The natural scientist looks for and claims to find discrete countable objects: stars, atoms, molecules, chromosomes. The chemist trying to determine the structure of a protein wants to identify the number, kind, and sequence of distinct objects that are linked together to form the more complex object. The world of thought and action is not one of comparable discrete countable objects.[41] Describing a person's beliefs and attitudes, desires and expectations, and hopes and fears is not enumerating a collection of discrete items somehow associated in a mind. The course of a life does not consist of a sequence of discrete countable deliberations, decisions, and actions. We can segment a life into such a sequence, but we can do it in any number of ways. The joint undertakings of groups of people are not sequences of distinct countable transactions: contests, competitions, cooperations, conflicts, arguments, collaborations. We can segment them into such sequences, but in any number of different ways.

Collective phenomena like revolutions, protest movements, riots, panics, fads, and fashion are all notoriously resistant to precise location of beginnings and endings, participation and nonparticipation. The social groups of interest to us are unstable, shifting, and indefinite. Attempts to determine the precise composition of the class of intellectuals, or scientists, or the poor, or criminals, or the creative, or the middle class end in selection of one or another from an endless supply of arbitrary ways of drawing boundaries or in ceasing the attempt at precise specification of the class. Similarly one can define the classes of followers of a party or a doctrine, audiences for mass media presentations, contributors to a collective undertaking (such as scientific inquiry)—but only by arbitrarily drawing boundaries. Historians cannot do without time periods, but history does not fall neatly into periods ending on one day, starting on another; one selects and imposes a periodization. Large-scale social and economic and political structures are not independent identifiable items within society but patterns abstracted from the flux of impermanent and imprecisely determinable relations of individuals and groups. Different individuals will find equal warrant for finding different structural patterns. Basic social phenomena like power, influence, authority, status, convention, custom, norm, and standard are phenomena of widely varying elasticity and indefiniteness, with manifestations in behavior that are as numerous and ambiguous as the manifestations of belief and desire. The things one deals with in history and the social sciences are in varying degrees and ways evanescent, impalpable, flickering, elastic, fluid, indefinite, kaleidoscopic—all metaphors for a world quite unlike a world of hard, stable objects.

It is the peculiar character of the phenomena of interest to the human studies that explains the perpetual confusion of terminology in those studies that might otherwise be attributed to lack of discipline and rigor. The same thing explains the difficulties of classification in the human studies and the perpetual popularity of the ideal type in social description—the imaginary pure case that may be exactly exemplified nowhere. We can apply the hard-soft dichotomy to classification as to objects and fields of inquiry. The classical ideal of a hard classification is that of the partitioning of a universe of objects into mutually exclusive and jointly exhaustive classes, based on the application of precise rules, in the form of necessary and sufficient conditions for class membership, which assign every individual to exactly one class.

In attempting to sort out social phenomena, it is impossible, or possible only by dint of numerous quite arbitrary decisions, to achieve a satisfactory hard classification. Instead one operates in a fluid and ambiguous situation in which any or all of the following features may be found. First, there may not be a well-defined collection of items to be classified. The items may constantly change character and shape, may not even be clearly distinct from one another, may merge into one another, expand or contract, appear and disappear, wax and wane. Second, one may be unable to arrive at rigorous defining conditions; instead there may be a variable number of type specimens, or shining instances, real or imaginary, that define a class by example rather than by verbal definition. Third, individual items to be classified may not unequivocally belong to a class but be more or less clearly associated with it and perhaps with two or more classes. Assignment to a class may be not a matter of applying a rule but of judging, without a rule, that an item is sufficiently similar to a type specimen or to other items already associated with that type. Finally, the classification may be incomplete; items that do not sufficiently fit into any class may be left unclassified or assigned to a special class of nondescript items. The more of these features one finds oneself confronting and the more pronounced each feature is, the softer the classification.

Soft classification violates the traditional rules of classification, but it is endemic to social inquiry because of the nature of the phenomena being classified. Ideal or constructive typologies are splendid examples of soft classification. One uses them in the expectation that nothing will fit exactly, that many things will fit equally well at several places in the typology, and that some things may not fit anywhere. In practice they seem indispensable in social description, as they have been for thousands of years.[42]

Any soft classification can be hardened, as any hard classification can be softened. One is likely to think of the recipe for hardening a soft classification as that of defining one's terms, providing operational definitions, and the like. But what does one do if the objects to be classified are themselves soft? One can eliminate all but those that meet some criterion of stability and clarity of boundaries or one can tailor the objects so they will fit neatly into a category. Those are both ways of changing the subject. Substituting a collection of well-defined objects for a collection of amorphous and indefinite ones is a way of putting oneself not in a position to talk precisely about one's original objects but to talk about a different group of objects. We are not always interested in doing that. Why should we be? But certainly much effort in the social sciences has gone into attempts to produce hard classifications of social phenomena as a prelude to discovery of strict laws governing thought and action. The persistent failure of the search for laws suggests that social phenomena may have to be recognized as incorrigibly soft. There will always be ways of hardening soft classifications, though no one of them will be decisively and demonstrably superior to the others. But then everyone is free to employ his own favorite version of a classification, hard or soft. That is the situation in history and the social sciences.

It is no wonder that the human studies should provide an endless number of different approaches to the same subject matter, that different people should choose different ways of dividing up the social world, that agreement on the application of concepts should be so hard to obtain, that terminology should be a permanent muddle, and that multiple interpretations of the same or nearly the same division of subject matter should be ubiquitous.

Fashion Revisited

Earlier we raised the question whether fashion played the same role in all branches of the knowledge industry. It is tempting to think that fashion is more important in the human studies than in the natural sciences. Our discussion of soft classification is relevant to the question. We cannot hope to settle it but may provide a plausible case for one answer.

In the natural sciences, there is a pragmatic test of success that is generally not available in the human studies. The test is prediction. The natural scientist may be free to choose what to study, but nature may not oblige by giving reproducible results and successful predictions. The theories and experimental procedures employed work or do not work; success may often be ambiguous and indeterminate, but it is not always so. New equipment and new procedures can be seen to give better results, conferring more power to explain and predict in controlled experimental circumstances. Much of the constant change in direction and style of inquiry can be explained in such terms without recourse to changes of intellectual taste.

By contrast, in the human studies, there is no comparable test that would enable one to choose among competing styles of inquiry. The same social phenomena can be described and interpreted from different perspectives and in different styles. The alternatives for the historian or social scientist are like those for the artist. Different artists painting the same landscape will produce startlingly different pictures: realistic or romantic, abstract expressionist, symbolist, formalist. The same external world allows a myriad of representations of the world seen from different distances and angles, through different kinds of lenses and atmospheric effects.

Each of the social sciences provides a range of different theoretical perspectives on the same social life, and there are plenty of mixed perspectives. Even from a single perspective there are unlimited ways of hardening the soft classifications that form part of one's initial conceptual scheme or theoretical perspective and of constructing one's description and interpretation of a chosen scene. This is not to say that one work is as good as another one written from the same perspective or that one perspective is as good as another. But there is no decisive test for the superiority of one theoretical perspective or one style of work. Of course, one's work must be consistent with and take into account all the relevant facts but this constraint is not an especially onerous one, for facts are malleable. There are always either too few facts to rule out many of a large number of alternative descriptions, or too many of them to be usable in totality, so one must select, being constrained not by the world but by one's own rules of relevance. What kinds of facts to take into account, how seriously to take them, and how to take them are matters settled not by tests of predictive success but by intellectual taste. Choices of perspective and of the style of research are decided on the basis of intrinsic satisfaction. It is by no means necessary that change of taste be rapid in lines of inquiry where external tests of success are unavailable and external constraints relatively light. But almost necessarily taste will explain more of what change does occur in such fields than in fields subject to pragmatic tests of success. Fashion rules in such fields because there is nothing else to rule except convention, which is simply "long lasting fashion."[43] Even in natural science, we might expect it to dominate in the descriptive and historical parts. And in the formal sciences, unconstrained by the natural world, it has been claimed that the mathematician's "criteria of selection, and also those of success, are mainly aesthetical"—that is, based on appeal to intellectual taste.[44]

Critical Authority

It is by now a commonplace among educated people that questions of fact need to be distinguished carefully from questions of value, and that one cannot expect to resolve questions of value simply by settling questions of fact. And it is widely thought that questions of value are by nature always open. They cannot be settled since they are basically expressions or reflections of personal preferences, which differ and cannot be expected to converge. For some people, this may imply that people can have cognitive authority in questions of fact but not in questions of value. Nothing is further from the truth. We are likely to rely most on our cognitive authorities when we need advice on questions of value. We need to know who is doing good work and who is doing bad work; what is worth giving our attention to in the realms of music, pictorial art, literature, social thought, politics; and what we should do and strive for. We all recognize some people as better sources of advice on such questions than others; we have cognitive authorities in value spheres. They are the critics whose judgments carry extra weight for us and may carry enough weight to settle questions of value for us, if not for anyone else.

It is no more true that questions of value are always open. They can be closed and agreed to be closed. All it takes is for people to come to agreement on a common opinion and to conclude that all that need be said on the question has been said and that further argument or examination is unlikely to make any difference. "Settled" means settled for all practical purposes. And questions of value not only can be but in fact are settled. In this society, for example, it is settled that slavery and torture are not tolerable. Not only are the questions of slavery and torture settled, but it is settled *that* they are settled; we share a common cognitive stance in the matter.

Contrary to what might have been expected then, we can consider criticism as a branch of the knowledge industry. The production of works of criticism is as much a proper part of that industry as is the production of works of theoretical natural science or history. But it is also clear that there is no question of the industry's claiming exclusive jurisdiction over criticism in general. Everyone engages in critical evaluation; we are all critics, though mostly not critical authorities for anyone else. In particular, there is no critical institution with a plausible claim to institutional authority in matters of criticism, but there might have been. It might be recognized, for example, that a certain closed and self-perpetuating group of literary critics are the authorities on questions of literary value. It might be the special office of such a critical establishment to establish a canon of serious works of literature, to assign ranks in the canon to individual works of literature, to screen new works and collectively decide which ones to admit to the canon and which to reject. New members of the establishment would become such simply by being recognized by old members as having proper taste and superior discrimination along with adequate familiarity with literature both canonical and noncanonical.[45] Or membership might be a formal matter of election. The establishment would be the arbiter of taste. If one aspired to have taste in literature—that is, good taste—one would have to get one's own taste and judgment to conform to theirs.[46]

There is no difficulty about the notion of a critical establishment, in literature or any other cultural realm. The question is whether such establishments exist here and now. The answer is surely that they do not. The very idea that to have taste in music or literature one must share the judgments of a critical establishment now seems wonderfully old-fashioned. Widespread deference to professional critics of literature and other arts has apparently disappeared, and the literary critics are in disarray. That may be only a temporary condition. Nothing in the nature of things or the nature of value excludes the possibility of future critical establishments with generally recognized authority.

But for now, we will not even bother to submit to our jury a case for the institutional authority of critical establishments. The case would have no chance of winning. Critics of literature, art, music, film, dance, architecture, and society must get whatever authority they can by their reputations and the persuasiveness of what they say, not by their standing in an authoritative critical institution.

There remains a crucial question for our jury to consider: the question of specialists in the knowledge industry having a monopoly over criticism of their own work. Peer evaluation is at the basis of the organization and functioning of the industry, and specialist groups claim not only the first right of judging their own productions but also the final right. But the claim is disputed by those who have to judge the utility of the specialists' work for outsiders, by those who have to decide which specialty groups deserve support, and by others who claim the right to evaluate from the standpoint of an interested observer. Suppose the question of specialists' monopoly on legitimate criticism was put to our jury. What kind of argument might be made for the monopoly principle that might persuade the layman?

The obvious argument would be that the only serious criticism is informed criticism and that informed criticism in science and scholarship requires an understanding of the work evaluated that can be acquired only by doing similar work oneself. The only understanding that is adequate for criticism is that possessed by the expert. Thus only physicists can critically evaluate work in physics, only historians can critically evaluate work in history.

This argument is persuasive until one reflects that criticism of performances in research, as in art, requires the application of standards or criteria of good performance and that insiders' standards and criteria are not the only ones available. More carefully, criticism is an exercise of taste: intellectual taste in the case of research, artistic taste in the case of works of art.[47] Poets and composers no doubt feel that only they are qualified to judge their own works and those of their fellow artists; they believe the taste of the professional critics is flawed and distrust it. Only a practitioner can evaluate the work of another practitioner. We reject their claims. Why should we accept the scientist's or scholar's analogous claim? The claim that the performer's standards are the only proper standards, that what matters to the performer is all that matters, is as suspicious in the one case as in the other.[48] We do not admit that only a poet can judge poetry. Why should we admit that only a historian can judge works of history or that, more specifically, only a specialist in colonial history can judge a work of colonial history?

What we expect of an authoritative critic in any field is a proper taste, expressed in what we recognize as an appropriate set of standards and criteria of value and in superior discrimination in applying them to particular performances or to entire groups of performances. However discriminating, a critic gets no authority if the standards he applies are thought inappropriate. However appropriate the standards, the critic gets no authority if the application is thought clumsy. What the critic is expected to know about the matter criticized is simply whatever is required to allow discriminating application of appropriate standards. The music critic is expected to know about music, the critic of history to know about history. But how much must they know, and what sort of knowledge must they have? It may be a degree of expertise equal to that of the most outstanding specialists, or it may be only what an intelligent layman can gather by careful examination. It depends on what is being looked at and for. If what is being looked for is the quality of the research as it would be judged by the most subtle member of the specialty group itself, then the critic must have equal expertise as the group itself judges expertise. But if what is being looked for is something else—intrinsic interest, importance in altering the available picture of the world, practical significance, for example—then the insiders' evaluations may be irrelevant, and the critic may do without a technical understanding of the research performance equal to that of the insiders. Performers' criteria may differ sharply from observers' criteria. The expert's knowledge does not give weight to his critical judgments if we feel that his criteria of evaluation are inappropriate. And the principle of evaluative specialization will be accepted only by those who are persuaded that only performers' criteria are appropriate.

What is the situation then? The principle of evaluative specialization appears to be widely accepted. Specialists apologize for presuming to criticize work outside their own specialties and defer to others who can claim expertise. It is a "piece of etiquette which decrees that no specialist shall bother with the concerns of another, lest he be thought intruding and be shown up as ignorant."[49] The principle is not universally accepted, and if the arguments pro and con were put to the imaginary jury, it might well be that the principle would be rejected, and specialties not granted exclusive jurisdiction over questions of the value of their own work. Even so, the consequences of wide acceptance of the principle are visible around us.

It is worth pausing to wonder why there are occupational specialists in literary, music, art, drama, and architecture criticism but not in knowledge criticism. Inquiry as practiced by scientists and historians is a form of art; performances at research and writing would seem to be as suitable objects for public criticism as are performances in the arts. Criticism there is aplenty, but by specialists for specialists. Some works of history are reviewed in periodicals addressed to the layman, but the reviews are occasional pieces by people whose main work is elsewhere. There are specialized science reporters, but they describe and do not criticize. Critical reviews of progress in different fields of inquiry are regularly produced, but by specialists for specialists.

Occasional critical surveys of entire disciplines are written, usually by enthusiastic insiders who have nothing but praise for the discipline's achievements, and often meant as propaganda on behalf of the discipline, to encourage greater financial support from outsiders. The independent public critic of knowledge is nowhere to be found.

The absence of any recognized role for the independent public critic of knowledge lends support to Jacques Barzun's claim that "science and the results of science are not with us an object of contemplation . . . that is, of direct, unscholarly, unpedantic enjoyment, discussion, and criticism."[50] To make science an object of contemplation, Barzun notes, scientists would have to "begin the specialized work of organizing their ideas and finding a critical vocabulary for them" as has been done for other fields of cultural activity. Science is a proper subject for popularization: laymen can at least be told a little about what scientists are doing. But it is not thought a proper subject for public criticism; who would listen? If one accepts the principle of specialization, it is clear why one would think there are not and cannot be independent public critics of knowledge who take it as their business to criticize where they are not expert. If one rejects that principle, then the lack of public critics represents an odd social lacuna. The empty spot in the social array of knowledge occupations might have been filled by philosophers, and indeed, philosophers may think of themselves as those best fitted to serve as critics of the work of other branches of inquiry.[51] But philosophy itself is now one specialty among others and addresses itself as little to the public as do the scientific specialties. So we are left with no sustained public critical discourse addressed to the layman concerning those activities that are our outstanding cultural achievements.

Knowledge Production?

We have divided the knowledge industry into three large sectors: science (formal and natural), history (current and past), and criticism. Having initially put aside the sector devoted to the improvement of technology, we can now reintroduce it as the fourth major industry sector. Now we can summarize the situation with respect to the question whether the knowledge industry is recognized as producing knowledge.

It became clear early in the discussion that the individual publications reporting on work in the industry could not in general be regarded as containing or representing contributions of knowledge. At best they should be seen as contributing to knowledge, but many fail to do even that. Now we move from the individual publication to the entire industry sector. Are all sectors knowledge producers? Taking our imaginary jury and its verdicts as the criterion, we have the result that the natural and formal sciences are recognized as knowledge producers. Criticism is not so recognized. History is recognized as a producer of knowledge of elementary facts but not of interpretations or explanations of facts. Technology, we may assume, would be recognized as productive of new practical knowledge.

That part of the industry is recognized as producing knowledge means that the workers in that sector are considered to be collectively able to settle questions within their sphere. It is a general recognition of group competence. It implies no particular views as to what precise questions have been settled or what the answers are. And it says nothing about the amount of cognitive authority that any individual may have. It is directed at the cognitive standing in society of whole groups, not of individual members of the group. It can easily happen that an individual member of a group that lacks institutional authority might have great authority as an individual, those who encounter the individual or his works being mightily impressed by him though not by his group. And an individual member may fail to be recognized as having much, if any, cognitive authority though he belongs to a group that has it.

The result depends on the verdicts of an imaginary jury, and one might wonder how one could put any reliance at all on such a flimsy device. Let us recall the situation into which the device is introduced. Numerous groups of specialists make claims of this sort: "Take it from us, we know what we're doing, and you can believe us when we tell you what we've found. We are the experts in this area, and others' opinions about questions in our area should be treated as amateurish." Few people ever have the occasion to reflect carefully on such claims. We learn little about people's views from public opinion polls, and what we learn probably reflects no careful deliberation. Short of conducting massive and intensive field studies, we can only guess what would be the result if people were to engage in serious reflection on claims to institutional authority. The device of the imaginary jury is introduced to focus attention on a situation that would encourage careful deliberation and to help us arrive at good guesses. Whether the results of actual jury deliberations would resemble those sketched here is an open, empirical question. Even if actual results resembled our estimated results, other sorts of procedures of inquiry, asking other questions, might well produce different and even inconsistent answers. Public opinion is indefinite and malleable; there is no definite answer to the question, "What do people think about so and so?" independent of particular contexts of inquiry.

No use was made in the imaginary presentations to the jury of the notion of fashion. It seems likely that the finding that a sector of the knowledge industry was significantly influenced by the play of fashion would weaken, and at any rate certainly not strengthen, its claims to cognitive authority. Whether it should do so is something for each of us to decide.

Everything depends on our use of the word *knowledge*. We have purposely used it in a nontechnical, familiar, everyday sense, reflecting the crude distinction between what one considers closed and open questions. With a different understanding of the word, one would come to different conclusions about the production of knowledge.[52] One might prefer to say that knowledge is produced only when a question is closed for good, when at least one person is convinced a question has been closed, or when some favored group has been so convinced. And one might say it has been produced only when certain technical conditions, which one enumerates oneself, have been met. The possibilities are endless. One of the possibilities, however, we have meant to reject entirely: that we simply let each specialist group decide for us whether they produce knowledge and deserve recognition as cognitive authorities.[53]

Notes

1. See discussion of this in Fritz Machlup, *Knowledge and Knowledge Production* (Princeton: Princeton University Press, 1980), Ch. 3.

2. "Poll Says Scientists are Trusted Most," *San Francisco Chronicle*, 18 November 1981, p. 4. (A report on a poll by the Field Institute.) See also Amitai Etzioni and Clyde Nunn, "The Public Appreciation of Science in Contemporary America," *Daedalus* (Summer 1974): 191-205; "Public Attitudes toward Science and Technology," *Science Indicators 1976: Report of the National Science Board, 1977* (Washington D.C.: National Science Foundation, 1977), pp. 168-82; Dorothy Nelkin, *Science Textbook Controversies and the Politics of Equal Time* (Cambridge: MIT Press, 1977), appendix 2, pp. 164-66.

3. James B. Conant, *Science and Common Sense* (New Haven: Yale University Press, 1951), Ch. 3.

4. John Ziman seems to think that what distinguishes scientists from nonscientists is that scientists aim at consensus. This seems completely wrong. What distinguishes scientists is that they often achieve what others aim at but fail to achieve. See Ziman, *Public Knowledge: The Social Dimension of Science* (Cambridge: Cambridge University Press, 1968).

5. John Venn, *On Some of the Characteristics of Belief, Scientific and Religious, Being the Hulsean Lectures for 1869* (London: Macmillan, 1870), p. 4: "Our main reliance must surely be found in the fact that the genuine students are in substantial agreement. If they coincide in their conclusions, we do not doubt that they have arrived at least at some substratum of truth; if they are still in dispute, we mostly withhold our full assent from any one of them."

6. Scientists often complain that laymen do not, or cannot, distinguish between science and technology. The complaint does not deserve to be taken very seriously. The distinction is one that is much debated even within the scientific community, particularly in the way of trying to draw the lines among pure science, applied science, and technology. More important is the fact that for the outsider, technology is the most obvious demonstration of the competence of the institution of science. The only performances that the layman is likely to encounter that support the authority of science are technological performances. We take new technology as manifesting the power of science, and the continued grant of authority to science rests in part on continuing manifestations. This may be a mistake, and would, of course, have been a mistake a couple of centuries ago, when technology did not rest on science. If so, it amounts to another illustration of authority resting on misunderstanding.

7. Cf. Barry Barnes, *T. S. Kuhn and Social Science* (New York: Columbia University Press, 1982), p. 90: "In conjunction with the rest of society, they [scientists] must decide what is a scientific field and what is a pseudo-scientific one, what is a properly scientific argument and

what is not, what science can pronounce upon and what it cannot. And such decisions relate to issues of great moment, concerning which expert is to be believed, which institutions are given credibility, where cognitive authority is to lie, and ultimately what kind of society we are to live in."

8. See the "Specialties List for Use with 1970 National Register of Scientific and Technical Personnel," *American Science Manpower 1970, A Report of the National Register of Scientific and Technical Personnel* (Washington, D.C.: National Science Foundation, 1971), pp. 252-58. See also *Science Indicators 1976*.

9. Christopher Jencks, "Destiny's Tots," *New York Review of Books*, 8 October 1981, p. 32; Irving Kristol, quoted in T. W. Hutchinson, *Knowledge and Ignorance in Economics* (Chicago: University of Chicago Press, 1977), p. 36.

10. Paul Lazarsfeld, "Sociology," in *Main Trends of Research in the Social and Human Sciences, Part I: Social Sciences* (The Hague: Mouton, 1970), p. 90. See also Richard J. Bernstein, *The Restructuring of Social and Political Theory* (New York: Harcourt Brace Jovanovich, 1976); Stanislav Andreski, *Social Science as Sorcery* (New York: St. Martin's Press, 1973); A. R. Louch, *Explanation and Human Action* (Oxford: Blackwell, 1966); Ernest Nagel, *The Structure of Science* (New York: Harcourt, Brace, 1961).

11. Quentin Gibson, *The Logic of Social Enquiry* (London: Routledge & Kegan Paul, 1960); George C. Homans, *The Nature of Social Science* (New York: Harcourt, Brace, 1967).

12. Oskar Morgenstern, "Thirteen Critical Points in Contemporary Economic Theory: An Interpretation," *Journal of Economic Literature* 10 (1972): 1163-89; see also Wassily Leontief, "Theoretical Assumptions and Nonobserved Facts," *American Economic Review* 61 (1971): 1-7; Hutchinson, *Knowledge and Ignorance in Economics*; Lester C. Thurow, "Economics 1977," *Daedalus* (Fall 1977): 79-94. This list could be enormously expanded.

13. Jerome R. Ravetz, *Scientific Knowledge and Its Social Problems* (Oxford: Clarendon Press, 1971), pp. 367-68. Ravetz's chapter on "Immature and Ineffective Fields of Inquiry" (pp. 364-402) deserves careful reading by social scientists.

14. Bernard Berelson and Gary A. Steiner, *Human Behavior: An Inventory of Scientific Findings* (New York: Harcourt, Brace & World, 1964).

15. Ibid., p. 417.

16. Homans, *Nature of Social Science*, p. 4.

17. George Cornewall Lewis, *An Essay on the Influence of Authority in Matters of Opinion*, 2d ed. (London: Longmans, Green, 1875), p. 31.

18. Seymour Martin Lipset, "Predicting the Future of Post-Industrial

Society: Can We Do It?" in *The Third Century: America as a Post-Industrial Society*, ed. S. M. Lipset (Stanford: Hoover Institution Press, 1979), pp. 2-35; Marc J. Roberts, "On the Nature and Condition of Social Science," *Daedalus* (Summer 1974): 47-64; F. A. Hayek, "The Theory of Complex Phenomena," in *The Critical Approach to Science and Philosophy*, ed. Mario Bunge (New York: Free Press, 1964), pp. 332-49.

19. This would be vigorously denied by many social scientists; see, for instance, the president of the Social Science Research Council, Kenneth Prewitt, "Usefulness of the Social Sciences," *Science* 211 (1981): 659. Prewitt goes so far as to claim that "it is through theories and intellectual constructs that the sciences realize their greatest potential." As examples of the theoretical accomplishments of the social sciences, he cites the concepts of gross national product, identity crisis, span of control and acculturation, among others. But concepts are not theories. It would be interesting to see what theories Prewitt would mention as the theoretical accomplishments of the social sciences. Much is now being written on the utilization of the results of the social sciences. See, for example, *Using Social Research in Public Policy Making*, ed. Carol H. Weiss (Lexington, Mass.: Lexington Books, D. C. Heath, 1977), and the journal *Knowledge: Creation, Diffusion, Utilization*.

20. The relevant literature is voluminous. For a starting point, see E. Fuller Torrey, *The Mind Game: Witchdoctors and Psychiatrists* (New York: Emerson Hall, 1972).

21. Fritz Heider, *The Psychology of Interpersonal Relations* (New York: Wiley, 1958).

22. Lee J. Cronbach, "Beyond the Two Disciplines of Scientific Psychology," *American Psychologist* 30 (1975): 727. Cf. Sigmund Koch, "Reflections on the State of Psychology," *Social Research* 38 (1971): 669-709.

23. Horace Freeland Judson, *The Search for Solutions* (New York: Holt, Rinehart & Winston, 1980), pp. 142-43; Ravetz, *Scientific Knowledge and Its Social Problems*, pp. 364-402. Cf. Spencer Klaw, *The New Brahmins: Scientific Life in America* (New York: Morrow, 1969), pp. 273-77.

24. "We know in part, guess in part, in part we are mistaken and in a large part we are simply ignorant. Being in a mental state entails nothing about our awareness of that state." D. M. Armstrong, *A Materialist Theory of the Mind* (London: Routledge & Kegan Paul, 1968), p. 115. Cf. Richard E. Nisbett and Timothy De Camp Wilson, "Telling More Than We Can Know: Verbal Reports on Mental Processes," *Psychological Review* 84 (1977): 231-59.

25. Many historians would deny that biographers are historians. They prefer a narrow concept of history; I prefer a wide one.

26. Carl Becker, *Everyman His Own Historian: Essays on History and Politics* (New York: Crofts, 1935).

27. Maurice Mandelbaum, *The Anatomy of Historical Knowledge* (Baltimore: John Hopkins University Press, 1977), pp. 18-19.

28. Jacob Burckhardt, *The Civilization of the Renaissance in Italy* (New York: Harper, Harper Torchbooks, 1958), 1: 21. Cf. Emmanuel B. Le Roy Ladurie, "Recent Historical 'Discoveries,' " *Daedalus* (Fall 1977), p. 155: "It is all up to the creator: he leaves behind himself cultural monuments, elaborated out of vast and precious ensembles." Burckhardt said that "history is the most unscientific discipline; yet it contains much worth knowing." Quoted in Hans Meyerhoff, *The Philosophy of History in our Time* (Garden City, N.Y.: Doubleday, Anchor Books, 1959), p. 14. Meyerhoff ends his introduction with an unanswered "open question: in what sense is history a legitimate intellectual discipline?" (p. 25).

29. Jacques Barzun, *Clio and the Doctors: Psycho-History, Quanto-History, and History* (Chicago: University of Chicago Press, 1974), p. 101.

30. See, for instance, Allen Johnson, *The Historian and Historical Evidence* (New York: Scribner's, 1934).

31. Barzun, *Clio and the Doctors*, pp. 89-90.

32. Michael Scriven, "Truisms as the Grounds for Historical Explanations," in *Theories of History*, ed. Patrick Gardner (Glencoe: Free Press, 1959), pp. 443-75. Cf. Gordon Leff, *History and Social Theory* (University: University of Alabama Press, 1969); Geoffrey Barraclough, "History," in *Main Trends of Research in the Social and Human Sciences*, pt. 2, vol. 1: *Anthropological and Historical Sciences, Aesthetics and the Sciences of Art* (The Hague: Mouton, 1978), pp. 277-487.

33. David E. Stannard, *Shrinking History: On Freud and the Failure of Psychohistory* (New York: Oxford University Press, 1980), for a critical account.

34. H. Stuart Hughes, *History as Art and as Science: Twin Vistas on the Past*, World Perspectives, vol. 32 (New York: Harper & Row, 1964), p. 24. Cf. Barraclough, "History"; *History as Social Science*, ed. David S. Landes and Charles Tilly (Englewood Cliffs, N.J.: Prentice-Hall, 1971); Lawrence Stone, "History and the Social Sciences in the Twentieth Century," in *The Future of History: Essays in the Vanderbilt University Centennial Symposium*, ed. Charles F. Delzell (Nashville: Vanderbilt University Press, 1977), pp. 3-41.

35. See Cronbach, "Beyond the Two Disciplines of Scientific Psychology"; Gabriel A. Almond and Stephen J. Genco, "Clouds, Clocks, and the Study of Politics," *World Politics* 29 (1976-77): 489-522.

36. Clifford Geertz, "Blurred Genres: The Refiguration of Social Thought," *American Scholar* (Spring 1980): 165. Cf. *Interpretive Social Science: A Reader*, ed. Paul Rabinow and William M. Sullivan (Berkeley:

University of California Press, 1979); Robert Nisbet, *Sociology as an Art Form* (London: Oxford University Press, 1976).

37. Charles E. Lindblom and David K. Cohen, *Usable Knowledge: Social Science and Social Problem Solving* (New Haven: Yale University Press, 1979), Ch. 4.

38. Ibid., pp. 12-17.

39. See also Michael Scriven, "A Possible Distinction between Traditional Scientific Disciplines and the Study of Human Behavior," in *The Foundations of Science and the Concepts of Psychology and Psychoanalysis,* ed. Herbert Feigl and Michael Scriven, Minnesota Studies in the Philosophy of Science, vol. 1 (Minneapolis: University of Minnesota Press, 1956), pp. 330-39, esp. p. 338.

40. A good introduction to the controversy is found in Georg Henrik von Wright, *Explanation and Understanding*, International Library of Philosophy and Scientific Method (London: Routledge & Kegan Paul, 1971). The term *Geisteswissenschaften* was coined in 1863 to provide a German equivalent for what John Stuart Mill called moral sciences. Dilthey made the term current. See Ibid., p. 173. For an introduction to Dilthey, see W. Dilthey, *Selected Writings*, ed., trans., and introduced by H. P. Rickman (Cambridge: Cambridge University Press, 1976). Rickman (p. 12) notes that Dilthey used the term both for the study of mind in particular and the study of man in general; this is enough warrant for translating it back into English as "human studies."

41. Jean Piaget, "The Place of the Sciences of Man in the System of Sciences," in *Main Trends of Research in the Social and Human Sciences, Pt. 1: Social Sciences* (The Hague: Mouton, 1970), p. 27: "The chief difficulty with the sciences of man . . . lies in the absence of unities [units] of measurement"; Jacques Barzun and Henry F. Graff, *The Modern Researcher*, rev. ed. (New York: Harcourt, Brace & World, 1970), p. 248: "the chief inadequacy of social-scientific language stems from the absence of true units in the subject matter of the science." Andreski, *Social Sciences as Sorcery*, p. 20, stresses the "ubiquitous fluidity" of networks of human relations.

42. See John C. McKinney, *Constructive Typology and Social Theory* (New York: Appleton-Century-Crofts, 1966); Howard Becker, "Constructive Typology," in his *Through Values to Social Interpretation* (New York: Greenwood Press, 1968); Edward A. Tiryakian, *International Encyclopedia of the Social Sciences*, s.v. "Typologies." The locus classicus for the description of ideal types is Max Weber, "'Objectivity' in Social Science and Social Policy," in his *The Methodology of the Social Sciences*, trans. and ed. Edward A. Shils and Henry A. Finch (New York: Free Press, 1949), pp. 90-93. For a lovely ancient example, see *The Characters*

of Theophrastus, English trans. by R.C. Jebb, new ed. by J.E. Sandys (London: Macmillan, 1909). I will not attempt to steer the reader toward the vast quantity of literature in philosophy, logic, mathematics, computer science, and so on, that is relevant to formal attempts to deal with soft phenomena. The fuzzy set theory originating with L.A. Zadeh is one obvious instance.

43. Caroline A. Foley, "Fashion," *Economic Journal* 3 (1893): 461: "For the English language fashion is current usage; for the French *l'usage n'est qu'une longue mode*. Mode is *le goût mobile, usage passager*."

44. John von Neumann, "The Mathematician," in *The Works of the Mind*, ed. Robert B. Heywood (Chicago: University of Chicago Press, 1947), p. 194.

45. Patrick Wilson, "The Need to Justify," *Monist* 50 (1966): 267-80.

46. See Arnold Bennett, *Literary Taste: How to Form It* (New York: Doran, n.d.).

47. See the discussion of intellectual taste in chapter 3. Cf. Randall Jarrell, an admired critic as well as a poet: " 'Principles' or 'standards' of excellence are either specifically harmful or generally useless; the critic has nothing to go by except his experience as a human being and a reader, and is the personification of empiricism." Randall Jarrell, *Poetry and the Age* (New York: Vintage Books, 1955), p. 81.

48. Herbert Gans makes an analogous distinction in his *Popular Culture and High Culture: An Analysis and Evaluation of Taste* (New York: Basic Books, 1974), between "creator-orientation" and "user-orientation" (p. 62). So does Barzun: Jacques Barzun, *Science, The Glorious Entertainment* (New York: Harper & Row, 1964), pp. 26-27.

49. Barzun, *Science*, pp. 26-27.

50. Ibid., pp. 25, 27.

51. Karl Mannheim, "Competition as a Cultural Phenomenon," in his *From Karl Mannheim*, ed. Kurt H. Wolff (New York: Oxford University Press, 1971), pp. 259-60: "Epistemology would like to be taken for a critical science, whereas in fact it represents an underpinning and justifying sort of knowledge. . . . It demands to be recognized as an absolute standard, a tribunal, a critique, whereas in fact it is an adventitious structure, a mere system of justification for an already existing style of thought." See Richard Rorty, *Philosophy and the Mirror of Nature* (Princeton: Princeton University Press, 1979), p. 392, for a philosopher's attempt to convince other philosophers to "drop the notion of the philosopher as knowing something about knowing which nobody else knows so well" and "drop the notion that his voice always has an overriding claim on the attention of the other participants in the conversation."

52. Cf. Patrick Wilson, *Public Knowledge, Private Ignorance: Toward a Library and Information Policy* (Westport, Conn.: Greenwood Press, 1978). Public knowledge was defined there as "the view of the world that is the best we can construct at a given time, judged by our own best procedures for criticism and evaluation of the published record" (p. 5). It was clear that there would be problems if scientific groups themselves disagreed about what the best view was, and in such a case public knowledge would be indeterminate. Reflection on history and the social sciences shows us how considerable a problem that is. If there is no agreement among the experts on what the best view is, there is no public knowledge. It looks as though there is no public knowledge, in that sense, outside of formal and natural science.

53. Robin Collingwood was apparently prepared to accept just that possibility. He proposed to criticize psychology, but first asked himself: "But how are you going to examine the credentials of psychology? If the practitioners of a science claim that it gives genuine knowledge about its subject-matter, who is to tell them that they are wrong? They are the persons who study it scientifically, and they are the only persons who are qualified to criticise whatever passes for a scientific study of it. . . . if unscientific thought is permitted to pass judgment on scientific thought, the progress of science is at an end." He replies: "I accept the principle here appealed to. But I do not accept the professed application of it." For after all, logicians and metaphysicians have also studied thought. R. G. Collingwood, *An Essay on Metaphysics* (Oxford: Clarendon Press, 1940), p. 104. He concludes (p. 119) that psychology "as the science which tells us how we think" is a pseudo-science. By this line of argument, it looks as though psychologists, but no one else, could criticize metaphysicians and logicians. Those who claim to study a subject scientifically can criticize others who make similar claims, but no one else can. This is nonsense.

5 COGNITIVE AUTHORITY IN EVERYDAY LIFE

John, I can't make a damn thing out of this tax problem. I listen to one side and they seem right, and then God! I talk to the other side and they seem just as right, and there I am where I started. I know somewhere there is a book that would give me the truth, but hell, I couldn't read the book. I know somewhere there is an economist who knows the truth, but I don't know where to find him and haven't the sense to know him and trust him when I did find him. God, what a job.[1]

Warren Harding

Conflict and Conflict Avoidance

A small, homogeneous society might also be a unanimous society in matters of cognitive authority. In a unanimous society, everyone would know who the leaders are, who the priest or shaman is, who the teachers are, and everyone would have about the same ideas of what they can be expected to know. The Eskimo knows (or once knew) who the headman and the shaman are; the headman is *pimain*, "he who knows everything best," or *ihumitak*, "he who thinks," or *anaiyuhok*, "he to whom all listen." Among the Shoshone he is (or was) called *tekniwup*, "good talk thrown out to the people."[2] Such unanimity about cognitive authority is not impossible in a large, complex, heterogeneous society, but it is unlikely without strong and deliberate control over the formation and expression of opinion.

If the various spheres of possible inquiry are official monopolies of groups appointed or recognized by the state, if in each sphere the monopolists of opinion present a united front to the rest of the society, and if outsiders are forcibly prevented from expressing disagreement with the official views, questions of cognitive authority are closed, at least in the sense that it is not permitted to treat them as open. But they might be really closed, in that all members of the society agree on the competence of the various monopoly groups and on the appropriateness of taking their word as settling the questions arising in their spheres of influence. Cognitive authority in such a case, though backed by force, need not depend solely on force. In our times, such cognitive monopolies are likely to depend on force. The relative ease of communication means that it is difficult to conceal the fact that the world is full of competing claimants for cognitive authority. Awareness of the existence of alternatives is the first step toward weakening the hold of cognitive monopolies.

In a society in which inquiry and the expression of opinion is generally unrestrained, in which the results of past and contemporary inquiry are freely available, each individual is at least potentially faced with endless problems of cognitive authority. We do not have to go looking for others to instruct us; they come to us, through newspapers, magazines, and television programs, competing for our attention and acceptance. If we did want to go looking for them, the whole society—libraries, bookstores, schools, the halls of Congress—is full of those who would claim our acceptance as sources of knowledge. Competition is greatest in those spheres of most interest to most of us: the spheres of questions on how to live and what to do, as individuals and as societies. If we count not only what alternatives are currently available but also what have been available in the past and are still discoverable from written records, then the array of possible views on almost any question of importance to human beings is enormous. The question of whose views to take seriously is likely to produce bewilderment, confusion, or exhaustion. But this potential situation of uncertainty and bewilderment does not often arise. We have ways of avoiding the disagreeable problem of deciding whom to believe about what. We do not face the whole world of competing claimants for attention and acceptance, but only some tiny part of it; and we do not face it unprepared, but with minds already well armed with beliefs about who and what can be believed and with strategies for keeping the problem of choice among rivals within manageable levels of discomfort.

The Initial Stock

Any understanding of a particular individual's pattern of recognition of cognitive authority has to start at the beginning of life. Where and when a person started out in the world are the most important things about that person's mental life. Each person has the ideas of his own place and time, and if one set of ideas is discarded, it is only to adopt another set equally characteristic of place and time. However we struggle with our thoughts, what we laboriously work out is generally a trivial variant of ideas already available in our environment. This is as true for beliefs about others' knowledge as for any other sort of belief. The starting point is the best indicator of the ending point. At the start, one develops an initial stock of ideas about the world and also about how to enlarge it by drawing on others' stocks. One begins to learn very early who knows about what; one develops a stock of authority beliefs.[3]

A central part of one's stock of authority beliefs is knowledge about the social division of labor and the occupational structure, for that is knowledge about the distribution of specialized knowledge.[4] At first such knowledge is extremely sketchy and vague, but one acquires early some idea of what sort of person might be asked what sort of question, where the sorts are occupational categories. Another important and central part of the stock of authority beliefs consists of what we might call partisan knowledge. We learn that there are several competing religions, though only one of them has the truth, the others being in error, slightly or seriously. We learn that there are competing political parties and that one of them can be trusted but the others not. We learn that there is a class of businessmen who collectively know what is best for the country—or that those businessmen are capitalist enemies of the working class. We learn who are those who oppress us, who endanger us, who are enemies; and learning these things, we realize who can be believed and who cannot, for it is axiomatic that the enemy is untrustworthy. We get a more or less systematic introduction to conflict of authority: competing sources of opinions on the same subjects. This introduction raises and at once settles the problem of conflict by identifying the real authorities and the false authorities—the antiauthorities, those who can be reliably counted on to be wrong.[5] This introduction may last us for a lifetime: one religion, one political party, one social class may get and keep our allegiance for good.[6] Institutional authority is established early and may never be questioned.

In addition to such impersonal kinds of authority beliefs, we accumulate a set of individual authorities, starting with our parents. In the beginning, parents are not really cognitive authorities, as we are interpreting the notion of authority. They deeply influence the thoughts of the child, to be sure, but cognitive authority means influence that would be consciously recognized as proper, and this cannot come about until one develops the capacity to make the contrast between proper and improper. At first this capacity is wanting. It takes a while for the child to get to the point where there is any alternative to taking the parents' word, where doubt becomes possible. At that point, the child might not recognize parents as having cognitive authority, or at least as not having absolute or universal authority. Part of growing up is acquiring new and different authorities and part is a matter of gradually diminishing the sphere and degree of parental cognitive authority.

The other most important early cognitive influences are members of the peer group. Entrance into the period of life now called youth (formerly adolescence) is entrance into what is practically "a separate country, in which young people take out citizenship."[7] Parents may continue to have some cognitive influence over their children; teachers may have some, but "for the most part adults no longer have any significant sway over children."[8] Youth learns from other young people what seems at the time most important to know. This includes forbidden and dangerous knowledge (about sex and drugs, for example), and the kinds of things about which adults cannot be trusted to be knowledgeable: how to dress, how to behave toward peers. Who those peers happen to be, and what they think is worth knowing, are almost as much a given for the individual as who one's parents are. The influence of peers is as irresistible in youth as that of parents in childhood.

Except for schools, parents and peers are the major sources of one's initial stock of beliefs about the world, including one's authority beliefs. For our purposes, the most important thing about the initial stock is that it constrains the future by providing the body of beliefs against which the intrinsic plausibility of new claims about the world is judged. By the time one is ready to leave youth for adulthood, one's common sense is well developed; one's general picture of what the world is like, of what one can expect and cannot hope for, is settled.

All of these beliefs can change, but the processes of change will reflect the starting point. No one begins life by coolly comparing the merits of Catholic as against Protestant faiths, or of being an American rather than a German or a Peruvian Indian, or of believing in capitalism as against socialism. Whatever cool considerations of alternatives may later be undertaken, they are bound to differ in character depending on where one started. As one goes on, one's view of the world will change as one accumulates experience and learns from one's authorities. One's stock of authorities will change too as old ones disappear or lose authority, and as new candidates appear. Many, if not most, of those shifts can be explained by reference to the bases of authority already canvassed. What cannot be explained that way is the crucial question of how one comes to have the initial stock of beliefs that sets limits to future recognition of authority. Only the accident of birth can explain that.

Entrance Requirements

Growing up and trying to find a place for oneself in the world, one encounters successive entrance requirements for admission to desired social places and statuses, some of which are cognitive, others financial or physical or social. Schooling is a requirement set by adults for entrance into full independent adulthood. Evasion of the requirement or failure to meet it condemns one to inferior status. Teachers set various cognitive tasks; one must learn to perform in certain ways—read, spell, add and subtract, manipulate symbols in a style acceptable to the teacher. Whether one is interested in the material one is required to learn is irrelevant; so is the credibility of what one is set to learn—not that the question of credibility is likely to arise. A few of the young find the required performances easy, exciting, and interesting and they look forward to future opportunities to develop these cognitive skills that are so rewarding. For most, though, the performances are simply what one is required to do to meet the conditions for entry into adulthood or to prepare to meet the next set of entrance requirements.[9]

Aiming at entrance into college or university, one must study the subjects required for college entrance. Aiming at subsequent entry to a profession, one must study the subjects required for entrance into graduate study. There are required apprenticeships for crafts, examinations for civil service positions, examinations for admission to the bar, and so on. In all such cases, someone else is setting the tasks, saying: "This is what you have to do; these are the things you must remember and repeat on demand, and explain, defend, and manipulate in ways that we find satisfactory." Are those who set the tasks and evaluate performances recognized as cognitive authorities by those trying to pass the entrance requirements? Certainly what they say carries weight, but what kind of weight? The weight of the cognitive authority, who influences what one thinks about the world? Or the weight of the administrative authority, who can tell one what one has to do? For some, it must surely be the former; the teachers are recognized as having superior knowledge about the world. But for others, they are simply those who administer the entrance requirements for admission to desired places. One simply submits to their power, which is the power of exclusion. Wanting to move on to the next stage, requiring their approval for doing so, one learns what they expect one to say and tries to say it in ways they will approve. Whether one believes what they say is irrelevant, and explicit questions of cognitive authority can be avoided. One can be, and many students are, fundamentally indifferent to the content of the courses they take to satisfy various requirements for degrees and for entrance into further stages of their progress toward a desirable place. Once the courses are passed, their content is rapidly forgotten, though some traces or residues may remain.[10]

Professional education and advanced study in the sciences and social sciences and humanities require more than simple external conformity. One is expected to come to think and even feel in the proper ways, to accept fully the cognitive authority of the teachers, who are sensitive to signs of mere surface conformity and inner reserve.[11] But even if cognitive authority is ungrudgingly recognized, it still is based to some degree (no doubt very different for different individuals) on that social authority, the power of exclusion or of pushing one forward to especially desirable positions. Not for the last time in this chapter, we note the subtle and often ambiguous relation between cognitive authority and power.

Cognitive entrance requirements are not confined to schools and occupations. Admission to all sorts of positions and statuses requires demonstration that one has developed the ability to say, if not to believe, the right things. Admission to a religious community, a political or social group, seats of power and influence within various groups—all have more or less clear and definite cognitive entrance requirements in the way of appropriate beliefs, values, and skills. These can be met cynically. One can say, "I am going to find out what they expect one to think and then pretend to think that myself." But cynicism is not the rule. We have to recognize that a person who wants to be accepted by members of a group will tend to find what they say intrinsically credible, even though if said by others, it would sound incredible. The politically ambitious person can be sincerely persuaded of the reasonableness of doctrines and programs proposed by those whose approval he wants, which in other circumstances he would have ridiculed as impossible and unworkable. So we can understand the Marxian claim that the ideas of the ruling classes are the ruling ideas in society; those who want to join or serve the rulers find that the rulers' views are particularly persuasive.[12] This phenomenon illustrates the lability of the sense of plausibility, as well as the lability of taste in general, and intellectual taste in particular.[13] Ambition or desire for acceptance can open the mind in ways that lead to large changes in what we think plausible, desirable, interesting, and valuable, thus changing the body of prior belief and taste with which we will approach new situations and new candidates for cognitive authority. What we think plausible is influenced by where we want to be. What we come to think depends on what we want—not what we want to believe, but what we want to get.

Ordinary Work

Once out of school and at work, one faces new questions of cognitive authority, differing with the kind of work one does. For simplicity, we will consider only three sorts of work: ordinary work, professional work, and managerial work. Most of the jobs that people hold are informationally self-contained. Once one acquires whatever skill and information are demanded as entrance requirements for the job, there are only two further information requirements of the job: to take new instructions and to pay attention to what one is doing.[14] If questions that arise about what should be done cannot be answered on the basis of prior experience and prior instructions, one asks a co-worker or a superior in an administrative hierarchy. The administrative supervisor may indeed have a recognized claim to superior knowledge based on experience and training, the knowledge and skill expected of one in that position. But those in positions of administrative authority also control what are to be used as the working assumptions of a job, and these may be matters of decision rather than knowledge. The superior tells the subordinate: "You are to act on the assumption that . . ."; and even if the assumption is manifestly false, futile, or destructive, the subordinate is expected to act as if it were true, effective, and appropriate. The administrative authority has cognitive authority in this skewed sense, of having the right to give the official definition of the situation—the official line. He is a source of knowledge in that he settles questions for all practical purposes. Acceptance of administrative authority as being also cognitive authority is acceptance of an explicit or implicit injunction: If you want to succeed here, you must learn our ways of doing things and act on the basis of assumptions we supply. The desire to succeed may produce real, not feigned, acceptance of authority.

For every question that may arise within the informationally self-contained job, there is an established line to the cognitive authority that one is to accept at least outwardly. The worker may indeed bypass official channels, seeking information from unauthorized sources, but has no responsibility for acquiring information other than that from the administrative hierarchy. It is inherent in the work situation that the worker is supplied with just such information as he is thought to need and is expected to accept it without question. A worker may be required to submit to periods of retraining but does not have to select a trainer or decide what kind of training is needed. The job allows a certain cognitive irresponsibility; one does not need to ask who really knows what. Cognitive authorities come with the job.

Professions

The image still lingers of the professional as a person independent of any administrative authority and claiming cognitive authority in some sphere by virtue of arduously acquired esoteric knowledge. Doctors and lawyers working alone in private practice still serve as models of true professionals by comparison to whom the claims of other occupations to professional status are weighed. But the free professional exercising completely independent responsibility is not the typical professional, even if the ideal one. School teachers, engineers, nurses, social workers, and librarians typically work in organizations in which they are subject to administration direction, as do many scientists, doctors, and lawyers. Quite apart from questions of administrative authority, we ill understand the sorts of work commonly called professional by stressing independence. We do better to stress dependence.

Learning to be a professional requires learning what questions not to try to answer; it is learning to stay within limits. The professional is well practiced in deference— deference to members of other professions. The professional undertakes not to meddle in other professionals' business if they will not meddle in his. The professional's work is also informationally self-contained in the sense that what cannot be answered, done, or finished by use of his profession's stock of doctrine and tools is not his responsibility to answer, do, or finish. His responsibility extends only so far as the competence of his profession, and that competence does not extend to the ability to judge the competence of other professions or individual members of other professions. A problem with medical, legal, and financial aspects cannot be given to a doctor to solve, for the doctor will disclaim expertise in legal and financial aspects of the problem and will not undertake to inform himself by choosing other experts, judging the credibility of their advice, and proposing an overall solution. If he does this, he is not acting simply as a doctor, and he has no responsibility to act as anything but a doctor. He can remain irresponsible for any part or feature of a problem that he and his co-professionals define as being outside their scope. This is partly obscured by the fact that professionals like doctors and engineers often take on large administrative responsibilities, which force them to act not only as engineers or doctors but as generalist directors of affairs.

The professional can be irresponsible in another way. It is in the practice professions that the results of scientific inquiry and, in general, the work of the knowledge industry make contact with ordinary life. Medical practice incorporates new methods of treatment based on findings from biomedical research; engineers doing development work apply findings from physical science. The professions take advantage of theoretical progress to improve practice—designing and making new things, restoring health, and so on. So it appears that members of the professions have a responsibility for monitoring the output of the knowledge industry in a constant quest for applicable findings—and consequently that they constantly face questions of cognitive authority, having to decide whom and what they can trust in all the complexity of the knowledge industry and its output. Further, the conduct of daily work may require considerable search for trustworthy data. It is usual to say that maintenance of professional skill requires constant effort at acquiring new information about developments in the profession's body of technique and information. Finally, other professions may challenge the claims of one's own profession, and outside critics may question its competence. In theory the professional might seem to be faced with a huge and open-ended task of looking for relevant information, trying to evaluate the credibility of sources, examining the foundations of his profession, and the like. But in practice a professional can be as informationally passive as any routine worker. Indeed a profession is by purpose a cognitive routine: an established way of discovering and evaluating new ideas and new practices, of endorsing them, publicizing them, securing their dominance. For the ordinary practicing professional, the question of what and whom he can believe is settled by the profession; that is the very idea of a profession. The professional can maintain a studied indifference to outside judgment on the profession as a whole. It is not his responsibility to accredit the profession. He recognizes the cognitive authority of the group and accepts the official group doctrine that outsiders are incompetent to judge his work. The job of search of the external environment for relevant information can be delegated to other specialists, such as editors of professional magazines or compilers of reference works endorsed by leaders of the profession. Maintenance of professional skill can be accomplished by subscribing to one or two magazines published by the profession for its members or by refresher courses arranged or endorsed by the profession. Search for information needed in daily work can be confined to conventionally accepted sources and channels. The idea of a profession is the idea of a group with group-approved ways and means of acting within a sphere defined by the group. A professional accepts the received ideas of how the work is to be done. A profession may certainly have creative members, but creativity is not essential to professional status. Conformity is more nearly essential, as is complete acceptance of the cognitive authority of the profession as a group.

Increasingly, professionals work in complex administrative structures in which others control the official definition of the situation and the working assumptions of the job. The difference, if indeed there is any significant difference, between a professional and a technician will lie not so much in differences in formal education as in tightness of constraints under which one works. The technician will work more clearly at the direction and under the supervision of another, having little or no responsibility or opportunity to determine the choice and scheduling of work to be done. But the difference is one of degree, and one can speak of professional technicians, who are deployed by administrative superiors, doing the (often highly skilled) jobs they are told to do, working on assumptions given by others. The scientifically or technically trained worker in industry is often simply a production worker, whose work is almost entirely routinized.[15] The professional working in a large organization may be in effect simply a smart tool used by others at their discretion, and with no more real problems of cognitive authority than the holder of the most routine unskilled job.

The Direction of Affairs

Contrasting scientists with professional administrators, C. P. Snow remarked: "To be any good, in his youth at least, a scientist has to think of one thing, deeply and obsessively, for a long time. An administrator has to think of a great many things, widely, in their interconnections, for a short time. There is a sharp difference in the intellectual and moral temperaments."[16] The difference in temperament goes with a difference in the scope of responsibility. The manager's job is inherently open-ended, unlimited, and endlessly demanding. "The manager is responsible for the success of his organization, and there are really no tangible mileposts where he can stop and say, 'Now my job is finished.' "[17] The manager is perforce a generalist. The specialist professional can ignore everything in a situation defined as outside his professional province, but nothing can be outside the manager's province.[18] He cannot expect to know much at first-hand; he has to depend on second-hand knowledge. But he cannot escape the responsibility of locating trustworthy sources of relevant knowledge or of figuring out what is relevant. Questions of cognitive authority loom large in managerial work. Whom should one take as advisers?[19] How much weight is to be given to the claims of this and that professional group? Are there unrecognized groups and individuals with knowledge on which one should draw? Whatever affects the success of the enterprise is within the scope of the manager's responsibility, and fulfillment of that responsibility requires, in principle at least, a large and accurate picture of the entire world so far as it relates to his enterprise, and of the sources of knowledge from which detailed information can be gathered. The picture one draws cannot be a simple sum of details provided by different experts. The interrelations of the separate specialist perspectives and bits of detail have to be sorted out finally by someone not a specialist or not acting as a specialist. The cognitive responsibilities of the generalist manager, unlike those of the routine worker and the professional, are not avoidable by submission to administrative authority or to the institutional authority of a group.

Not everyone doing managerial work is in the position of the generalist top manager. Management jobs can be divided into specialties whose incumbents can be as narrowly focused as any professional or expert in the knowledge industry, and middle-level bureaucrats can limit their attention severely to narrowly defined responsibilities. Let us speak not simply of managers but rather of directors. The director of an enterprise is the one responsible for the entire operation, and with such responsibility comes the width of cognitive concern. The director is not the only one in such a situation; the same kind of situation is faced by anyone involved in the direction or planning or comprehensive criticism of affairs, in business, government, politics, any kind of public life. The business executive, the trade union leader, the chief of a professional organization, the members of a legislative body, the heads of a state, the director of a nonprofit organization, the social critic: all are, by the nature of their undertakings, faced with open-ended and undefined obligations to take into account whatever might seriously affect their conclusions or decisions. All depend on expert advice over wide ranges of matters lying outside their own personal experience. All must depend on sources of uncertain reliability and doubtful authority. All are likely to face conflicting stories and competing advisers. And all of them face the problems of deciding whom to believe and whom to trust armed only with the same sorts of bases for recognizing cognitive authority as everyone else has. There is no specialist art of solving that sort of problem.

In reality, the heavy cognitive requirements of the situation may be ignored or treated lightly. Directors may be ill informed and even contemptuous of those who seem to work too hard at being informed. The manager's job can be turned into a cognitive routine, governed by the managerial class's conventional wisdom, which may countenance a small and narrow view of one's situation. But it is hard to escape the view that the situation really does carry a recognized responsibility of an open-ended and nonspecialist sort. Howard Becker proposes a general law of the hierarchy of credibility: "In any system of ranked groups, participants take it as given that members of the highest group have the right to define the way things really are. . . . those at the top have access to a more complete picture of what is going on than anyone else. Members of lower groups will have incomplete information, and their views of reality will be partial, and distorted in consequence. Therefore, from the point of view of a well socialized participant in the system, any tale told by those at the top intrinsically deserves to be regarded as the most credible account obtainable of the organizations' workings."[20] The law has great plausibility as a statement of what one ought to be able to expect, for it is the recognized responsibility of leaders to attempt to maintain an adequate picture of the situation in which they act as leaders, and their position gives them access to information unavailable or available only with difficulty to others. This applies to political and administrative leadership in a state, as well as to leadership in an organization or a small community. If the leaders are ill informed or worse informed than are the followers, they are incompetent and do not deserve their positions. They may be competent, hence well informed, but dishonest, in which case they are not trustworthy sources of information. But if one supposes them both competent and trustworthy, then the hierarchy of credibility describes the normal and desirable situation.

The cognitive responsibilities of the generalist director place him in direct conflict with experts of all kinds in their pretensions to be the sole judges of their own competence and credibility. Specialists in the knowledge industry and professionals outside it claim to possess knowledge and skills that outsiders are incapable of evaluating properly. The generalist director is responsible for doing exactly what it is claimed he cannot do: evaluate the competence and value of the specialists' offerings. Everyone agrees that in running a complex organization or trying to solve difficult issues of public policy, the advice of experts is indispensable. Natural scientists and social scientists are called on to advise legislators and administrators; professionals of all sorts are needed to advise in planning and decision making. But every discussion of the use of expert advice from the point of view of the manager or decision maker stresses the inherent conflict between experts' and decision makers' views of the situation and responsibilities.[21]

From the generalist's point of view, the expert suffers from a trained incapacity to see issues and problems in perspective. The expert's advice tends to exemplify what Abraham Kaplan calls the law of the instrument: "Give a small boy a hammer, and he will find that everything he encounters needs pounding."[22] The academic expert is as irresponsibly committed to applying his own special skill and ignoring what will not yield to exercise of that skill as any other sort of professional. "The academic community . . . is barely able to pull up its socks and deal with any kind of complex public issue in a useful way. . . . The political scientist, sociologist, engineer, and economist want to treat the matter at hand in political, sociological, engineering or economic terms. But our world is not built that way. The college catalogue is a poor map of human affairs."[23] Analogous complaints are available from almost any generalist director, planner, or critic of affairs. The difference in perspective between generalist and specialist is of critical importance. The specialist in a director's position must change perspective or else fail. Not only must the director make corrections for the specialists' trained incapacity to think in any terms but those of their specialty; he must also judge critically the worth of the advice he receives. The production of new knowledge may be left to specialists, but its applicability has to be judged by those responsible for action, and this necessarily means deciding what weight, if any, to give to their claims. Elsewhere one may get along well without making a distinction between expertise and authority. The director who fails to make the distinction takes all expert opinion at face value and gets, not special commendation for wise modesty of judgment, but scorn as a fool. The specialist's claim to freedom from outside criticism fails completely when it comes to the point of advising others on the conduct of affairs.

Private Life

Away from work, we are all in the position of the generalist manager; the affairs to be managed are our own. One member of the household may be reduced to the position of the routine worker, relying on another member as cognitive or administrative authority to define the situation, supply the working hypotheses, and settle disputed questions. More commonly now, the management job is shared. Those with the responsibility face what is in theory a staggering series of problems of identification of authorities. Much of private life is devoted to basic maintenance—just keeping lives going at a tolerable level. Simply maintaining a particular level of life requires the help of a variety of specialists from time to time who can fix things for us, advise us on how to fix things, or help us stay out of situations that call for fixing. The specialists whose help we need are not biologists but doctors, not physicists but plumbers; at the higher levels of wealth, not literary critics but interior decorators and couturiers. There is the choice of schools for the young, medical care for all. Financial problems may call for expert advisers, emotional problems for help from someone—priest, friend, psychotherapist. The specialists are those who presumably have knowledge that we need, but what we actually need is its exercise on our behalf. Professionals are supposed to have complex esoteric bodies of doctrine; for the outsider, this is all hearsay and rumor. Ability to give good advice and perform valuable services is what is wanted, and the cognitive authority recognized is in virtue of presumed knowledge of what needs to be done and how to do it. Producing one's life is an intricate exercise in design and choice, and the varieties of specialized knowledge that might be utilized in the production are practically endless. The responsibility is enormous and cannot be delegated without resigning from the ranks of independent and complete individuals.

In practice, the identification of authorities seems for the most part to be done without much difficulty. Authorities are acquired casually and often quite accidentally. As life goes on and we settle into comfortable habits and routines, we assign different degrees of cognitive authority to our various friends, acquaintances, and co-workers, and we learn of the reputations of others not personally known to us. Accidental encounters continue, in personal acquaintance or through the mass media. Movement from place to place, physically or socially, disrupts old patterns of social relationship and leads to the formation of new ones, depending again on the accidents of co-location. We pick up authorities along the way through life, not searching for them but accidentally happening on them.

Nevertheless at times we do have to look for them. We need a lawyer suddenly and urgently but do not know the names of any lawyers. We feel as if we are going mad but are entirely unprepared with plans for coping with such a situation. How shall we find the right person to consult? One might have expected that people would try to identify the best available practitioner of the appropriate sort, assuming that at least one already knows what is the appropriate sort of practitioner to seek. One might expect that people would start by inquiring narrowly into the relative standing of different practitioners, their reputations, their successes and failures, their training, their fees. A newspaper columnist advises on how to choose a lawyer—"Ask to see briefs the lawyer has filed"—though she does not explain how to make sense of the briefs.[24] But there must be other ways of getting information that would help one make a reasonable choice, and the more serious the need, the more one would expect people to engage in a systematic search for information. In fact this seems to be exceptional. More commonly we select on the basis of a casual recommendation; a friend or acquaintance suggests the name of a doctor or lawyer, which we gratefully accept. Or we select a name at random from the telephone directory, or go to the nearest and most easily available office. If one doctor fails to help us, we go to another one. If medical doctors fail to help us, we switch categories, choosing to try acupuncture, herbalists, faith healers. We engage in trial and error experimentation almost at random.

Why are people not more rational in approaching problems of choice of authorities? There are at least two plausible explanations. First, the information we would need to make a careful, deliberate choice may be unavailable. Doctors are not going to tell us how successful they are, or if they do, we will not be able to believe them. Professionals are ready enough to judge each other privately but not to publish their rankings for all to see.[25] Nor do other kinds of experts—auto mechanics, for example, cannot be expected to provide us with credible self-rankings. Reputations among nonspecialists are hard to discover and may be ill deserved, and how do we know that a person with a good general reputation will be good for us? Reputation may have turned out in the past to be an undependable guide. The more desperate we are, the more urgently in need, the less time we have for search for information, but also the less sure we are that we really could expect that the information we might find would lead us to a good choice. So we may actually avoid information that might be available. "It hasn't helped them in the past, and they believe it probably won't help them now. They make a choice because it is a necessity. Their car won't run. They have a pain in their side. Their husband wants a divorce. So with no prior search or information processing, they look in the telephone directory."[26]

That is one explanation, and it is surely the right one in many cases. But there is another explanation for other cases. We may not be mistrustful of specialists, but on the contrary prepared to assume that any accredited member of an occupational specialization can be expected to have a basic competence in the work of the specialty. And we may suppose that our problem, which drives us to seek expert help, is probably a simple or even routine one, that would be within the competence of any member of the occupation, and that additional expertise would be unnecessary extra power, of no extra benefit. If we think this, it is not surprising that we should consult the first one we encounter. Since we think we have no need of the best practitioner, it would be time wasted to engage in inquiries aimed at finding the best (but uncertain to do so). So, oddly, both trust and distrust of specialists can lead to the same behavior: the trusting attitude being that one specialist is as good as another for routine cases, the mistrusting attitude being that one is likely to be as bad as another and that search for information will not help.

Mistrust of occupational specialists, including members of the various professions, seems to be an increasingly common phenomenon. One often hears laments about the loss of respect for authority, the decline of deference to expert opinion. But what seems to be happening is not a rejection of authority but rather a diminution of the amount of authority people are prepared to recognize in certain prominent groups.[27] Most of us have no occasion to need the services of any but a few sorts of specialists and have no opinions on the credibility of the practitioners of numerous relatively esoteric specialties. About doctors, lawyers, teachers, automobile mechanics, and plumbers, we do have occasion to form opinions. Our views are likely to depend on accidents of personal experience and conversation. A single unhappy experience with a lawyer or plumber may cause us to distrust all lawyers and all plumbers, and a single shocking story told by a friend may have the same effect.[28] On whatever slender basis of evidence, the complaints against those specialist groups most often consulted in ordinary life seem to mount: that they are overpaid and overspecialized, that they artificially stimulate demand for their own services and engage in needless or positively harmful work, that they monopolize simple practices that actually require no special expertise, that they are often incompetent and dishonest, that professional organizations are unable or unwilling to enforce minimum standards of performance, that their claims to knowledge and special competence are overblown, that in some cases they have no special competence at all. Teachers do not know how to teach, surgeons perform unnecessary surgery, psychotherapists can help people no better than an untrained layman. Such views do not imply that no one knows anything better than anyone else but that these particular groups of people deserve less cognitive authority than they claim and have received in the past. And while one might regret the prevalence of mistrust, it would be absurd to claim that people should ignore their own bases for mistrust and accept every self-pronounced expert as deserving a high degree of cognitive authority.

The World as Spectacle

The time remaining to us after sleep, work, and personal and household maintenance can be called elective time or free time. For some people, particularly professionals and managers, it is difficult to say when work time stops and elective time starts; most of one's activities are related in some way to one's work. But even so there is some amount of one's time whose expenditure is discretionary and can be spent in alternative ways; and for most people work time is fairly sharply distinguished from elective time. Some part, possibly a large part, of that elective time is spent on the acquisition of second-hand information from newspapers, television programs, magazines, books, conversation, and formal instruction. Some of this is the deliberate attempt to acquire useful knowledge or skill, to improve one's economic situation, upgrade one's work performance, make oneself less dependent on untrustworthy experts, and the like. But much of it is not so utilitarian in aim. For many of us, a good deal of time is spent gathering information in the activity best described as simply watching the world go by. The world is a spectacle, a great show, and watching it is an endless source of entertainment and instruction. We can do it seated in a café, watching television programs, looking out the window, reading newspapers, or traveling. It is a frequent complaint by critics of the mass media that television news is treated by its producers as a form of entertainment, not as a serious instructional form. The charge is correct but the blame is undeserved.[29] The game of world watching is a pure spectator sport. We decide which areas and facets of the world we want to watch, for how long, with what degree of attention. Of course, we can select only from what is offered us, but plenty is offered, in one medium or another.

Tastes differ wildly in this sport. One person may be amused by interesting trivia requiring only shallow emotional involvement, another absorbed in watching with profound emotional involvement the great public tragedies and high comedies of the world. As we distinguish between high culture and popular or low culture, so can we distinguish between serious world watching and light world watching.[30] Serious world watching is absorbed in things of apparently high historical importance; light world watching is attentive to small, local, or surface features of no great historical importance. Critics of the mass media blame them for appealing to a taste for light world watching and implicitly argue that everyone ought to engage in serious world watching, which is about as likely to happen as everyone's turning away from popular music to chamber music.

The difference between serious and light world watching goes with a difference in attitude to cognitive authority. The more serious and the more involved one's world watching, the more important is the authority of one's sources. This great event is terrible if what they say is true, but can we believe what they are telling us? The attitude is different in light and uninvolved world watching. It is not that truth and falsity are irrelevant but that the question of truth and falsity is not worth pressing. All stories presented as news stories carry the unexpressed major claim: "What I am about to tell you is, to the best of my knowledge, true." But the lighter the story and the lower our involvement, the less we are inclined to ask: "But how do I know it's true? Why should I believe this?" It does not really matter. One engages in light world watching for entertainment. News is often entertaining, and we do not even demand verisimilitude as we would if we were reading fiction.

Serious world watching is no more to be dismissed as mere entertainment than is listening in deep absorption to Bach's "Art of Fugue." It is a form of play, but a deeply serious one. Serious world watchers are clearly dependent on others for most of their information: journalists, political analysts, social commentators, politicians and statesmen, other observers and participants, propagandists. In the midst of things, no one can see enough to get a sure picture of what is happening. The reporter lacks the historian's advantage of knowing how events turn out. What makes serious world watching such a complex and subtle game is that it requires the construction of a picture of the world based not simply on partial information from doubtfully trustworthy sources but on information we can be certain is distorted and more or less intentionally misleading. We must constantly question the authority of our sources. But it is not so much their special competence at observation or reporting that we question but rather their honesty, ability, or inclination to avoid bias.

World watching need not be confined to the world of action. The world of thought is as eligible a subject for world watching as the world of action. We can approach a learned subject in two quite distinct ways: first with the object of mastery, second with the object of simple inspection. The would-be professional tries to master a body of doctrine or practice; he becomes skilled at the manipulation of doctrine. The spectator has a different aim, which is neither mastering a subject nor acquiring a new skill but rather simply learning what people say about the world. This too is world watching, but the part of the world being watched is the world of ideas, and it can be watched as one would view a complicated game. The point of this game is not to acquire new beliefs about the world, not to enlarge the stock of factual information; one need not raise or try to solve the question whether what people are saying is so or not, and one can simply put aside the question of authority. Of course, we want to be assured that they really are saying what we think they are saying, as in following the course of public events we want to be sure that the reports we are getting are reliable. But the question whether what they are saying can be believed is put aside; the play of ideas is watched simply as play. What cosmologists are saying about the origins and future of the universe, what philosophers are concerning themselves with, what the latest fashion is among the literary critics: the fact that people are proposing these ideas, telling these stories, worrying over these problems, can be treated as interesting displays of human behavior, fun to watch as the currents of thought move to and fro.[31] Like serious world watching, this is a game that appeals most to the sophisticated; it is not in the repertory of popular culture.

Public Issues

In an ideal democratic society, public matters would be outranked in importance to the individual only by private matters of basic maintenance and livelihood. First attend to personal matters of basic well-being, then attend to questions of how the group as a whole is to live its collective life. This is one kind of ideal of a democratic society: intense participation by all the people in the conduct of public life. In a large, complex society, participation cannot extend to voting on each issue; there are too many of them, and direct town-meeting democracy is out of the question. But selection of representatives should be accompanied by an understanding of public issues and of candidates' positions on the issues. The ideal carries with it the expectation of informed participation. Since the resolution of any significant public issue ideally requires careful consideration of the relevant available knowledge and opinion, and since no one can expect to be well informed by first-hand experience, consideration of public issues requires solution of weighty problems of cognitive authority. On any important issue, there will be at least two opposing positions, and often a bewildering number of positions, each occupied by a group of active protagonists.

We are faced with ranks of technical experts lined up on opposite sides. Each side brings forward its own authorities and seeks to discredit the opponents' counterauthorities. Even relatively small and local matters like zoning regulations and public school policies "call for specialists who debate technicalities and frequently confuse rather than clarify the issues."[32] Here the conflict of contenders for cognitive authority is open and seemingly unavoidable.

Ours is no ideal democratic society. We avoid the problem of choosing among competing experts supporting different positions by a variety of simplifying strategies. The simplest and most popular strategy is to ignore the conflict. We may simply not bother to participate, leaving that to the people who enjoy it.[33] We may participate at least by voting for candidates for office but choose a candidate simply on the basis of personal attractiveness or the plausibility of the candidate's statements. If we bother to vote on the issues put to the public for decision, we may form our opinions by drawing on our existing stocks of knowledge and opinion, without the trouble of inquiry or reflection. As students of public opinion have learned, people are willing to express opinions on matters about which they are entirely uninformed, and there is little inducement to inform oneself, for ignorant participation is not penalized.[34]

People are mostly inattentive to public questions, except in times of great emergency or great upheaval; private problems and private interests fully occupy their lives. A minority are attentive, interested in identifying important public issues and in arriving at more or less well-informed views. A still smaller minority are actively involved; they are candidates for office, campaign workers, lobbyists, public controversialists, or organizers of pressure groups. For the inattentive or barely attentive (another soft classification), politics and public debate are at best a spectator sport; opinions, when solicited, are based on little information or understanding, are inconsistent and fragile, representing no abiding conviction.[35] For the more attentive, questions of authority that might arise over particular issues are sidestepped by accepting the cognitive authority of an institutionalized source—party, church—or accepting the views of the group with whom one likes to be identified, or both of these at once. One's regular sources of information may provide opinions that can be taken without argument or inquiry. Tolstoy's Stepan Arkadyevitch has his contemporary analogues:

Stepan Arkadyevitch took in and read a liberal paper, not an extreme one, but one advocating the views held by the majority. And in spite of the fact that science, art, and politics had no special interest for him, he firmly held those views on all these subjects which were held by the majority and by his paper, and he only changed them when the majority changed them—or, more strictly speaking, he did not change them, but they imperceptibly changed of themselves in him.

Stepan Arkadyevitch had not chosen his political opinions or his views; those political opinions and views had come to him of themselves, just as he did not choose the shapes of his hat and coat, but simply took those that were being worn.[36]

This saves time. One's already established cognitive authorities advise one as to which other competing bands of authorities on a particular issue can be trusted and what is the appropriate cognitive stance to adopt toward the issue. If it happens that one's established authorities are divided on the issue or unable to suggest an appropriate stance, then one must choose among them or try to arrive at an independent conclusion. The choice among competing authorities is likely to be made on the basis of the test of intrinsic plausibility. The one whose position makes the most sense is the one chosen. There is still another basis for choice, of great importance. Whether what is said in favor of a position passes the test of plausibility, it will be rejected, and with it the authority of its supporter, if it leads to intolerable conclusions. It follows from this person's arguments for a position that we must give up hope of achieving social equality, say; but that would be intolerable; so his arguments have to be rejected and, with them, his claim to authority. If we cannot accept a conclusion or implication of the arguments for a position because it is morally outrageous or incompatible with important values and aspirations, we will reject the arguments, however superficially plausible they may be. Not only plausibility, then, but also consistency with our own values provides a test of cognitive authority. We cannot believe one who says implausible things, nor can we believe one who argues for intolerable conclusions. His stories may be correct so far as they go, but they cannot be the whole story. In a way, questions of authority in political (and moral) issues are easier to solve the more passionately we are committed to a position. Compatibility with a passionately held position is a sharp test of acceptability. The more deeply committed one is to a position, the more rapidly and ruthlessly one can reject claims to authority on the part of those proposing incompatible arguments or conclusions.[37]

If inconsistency with important values or views leads to rejection of claims to cognitive authority, it is clear (and familiar) that consistency with hopes and ambitions can lead to acceptance of cognitive authority. One who puts forward views and proposals that would favor us is sure of a sympathetic audience; one who offers help and hope to the oppressed, or who offers reasons for the continued predominance and prosperity of the favored, is sure of a hearing. If the bearer of bad news is avoided if possible, the bearer of glad tidings is welcome and treated with respect. This is true not only in matters of public issues but in private matters as well. We tend to be impressed by flattery, and its varieties are endless. Those who tell us how important we are, how underappreciated we are, how much we deserve what good things we have, how much we deserve more good things are all, in one way or another, flattering us. Ideologists are professional flatterers of one or another class of people, rich or poor.

Dependence on these two tests is likely to lead to charges of bias and ideological thinking. That political conservatives regularly find arguments by conservatives more compelling than arguments by liberals or radicals, and regularly suspect the adequacy of opponents' arguments that have implications they find intolerable, is sometimes treated as if it were a moral defect— or at the least a departure from rationality. It is indeed true that we all have a tendency to treat leniently those arguments we find acceptable and to criticize furiously those we find unacceptable, and to treat with different degrees of critical rigor arguments having acceptable and intolerable conclusions.[38] This is a natural defect against which we can try to take protective measures. And it is true that we often go on to suspect the motives and good faith of those who fail to pass the tests. We begin to think that one who puts forth such absurd arguments or who supports such totally inadmissible conclusions is in the pay of our opponents, paid to try to put a plausible face on an ulterior purpose that cannot be publicly revealed, or at least unconsciously influenced by personal or group interests. This too we can try to guard against. But there is no way of avoiding reliance on the two general tests if we are to choose among competing authorities in matters about which we do not think ourselves sufficiently informed to be able to come to independent conclusions. If that is ideological thinking, then ideological thinking is unavoidable when we have to rely on guidance from others.

Information Space and Small Worlds

We acquire our cognitive authorities in a variety of ways, only partly explicable by reference to the official stories we would tell if asked why we recognize those we do. Some, often the most important ones, we get in childhood, their authority practically an inheritance from parents, dependent on the accident of location in a particular time and place. Some, such as those in school, are almost forced on us. Some come with the job, where administrative authority carries cognitive authority with it. Some acquire cognitive authority from their power of exclusion, as when we find persuasive the things said by those whose acceptance we urgently desire. Some acquire it, and others lose it, by appealing to our hopes or affronting our strongest values. And some acquire it as a result of sheer accident; we happen on to people whom we find credible. Without deliberate search, we stumble onto those who may turn out to change our lives significantly. Predictable and unpredictable features of our life history present us with candidates for authority, which the background of prior belief and current circumstances lead us to accept or reject. But not merely which competing candidates will be accepted, but also which spheres in which we will be interested in candidates, needs to be explained. I am not interested in this person's claimed expertise in French provincial furniture. What is that to me? What does it matter whether he knows anything? But I am interested in another's claimed expertise in foreign policy, for he is being listened to by the government, and his influence on them may make a difference in my life and that of everyone else. So I do want to form an opinion on whether he deserves the authority he apparently has for the government. Authority in that sphere is of interest to me; authority in the furniture sphere of no interest. We all realize that people differ widely in the numbers and types of spheres that interest them and within which questions of cognitive authority seem serious. The differences are certainly very great, but there are patterns to be found if we look.

Reliance on second-hand knowledge depends on the sort of picture of the world that one tries to construct and maintain, and that is in part a matter of obligation and need to know, in part a matter of curiosity, choice, and desire to know. Between need and desire comes social convention. In part, the picture of the world that one constructs is what it is because though one neither needs nor especially wants to know certain things, one is expected to know them and would rather fulfill expectations than be blamed or scorned. Like the clothes one wears, the food one eats, the accent and vocabulary of one's speech, so also the things one is informed about and the questions on which one has views are influenced by social location. Ignorance of baseball and football scores and popular television programs would be thought very odd by large segments of the American working and middle classes, though it may be a badge of distinction among intellectuals. Wide knowledge of and interest in world events and world politics is not expected and not particularly admired by a majority of working-class people but is respected in the upper middle class. Knowledge of events and personalities in different cultural worlds is thought suitable or unsuitable depending on which world it is and which social class is concerned. Ballet is thought appropriate for people, particularly women, to be informed about by the higher classes, but not by the lower. Knowledge of stock car racing and professional wrestling is suitable in the lower but not in the upper classes. To be well informed is a virtue among all classes, but what constitutes being well informed varies with social location. An upper-middle-class person will think that to be well informed, one must know something of the content of traditional high culture and something of national and world politics but not necessarily anything of science, philosophy, or popular culture. If we test people's ability to produce information about high culture and world events, we find people very ill informed, but that is because we ask for information that we expect people like ourselves to have, not for information that others expect people like themselves to have.

What one needs to know also depends in part on what others expect one to know. What one needs to know in order to perform an occupational role or to fulfill one's obligations as a citizen participant in public affairs is set only in part, often a very small part, by technical requirements. What can be ignored and what must not be ignored are matters settled by collective agreements (tacit or overt) as much as, or more than, by the actual indispensability or dispensability of knowledge to performance. And finally, what one wants to know will reflect what one thinks others do know—what there is to know about. We cannot want to know about a certain sphere if we do not know that there is such a sphere to know about. In complex interaction, these factors of want, need, and others' expectations, along with opportunity and ability to learn, will affect the kind of picture we make of the world, its size, amount of detail, and accuracy.

It is possible to live a life almost free of reliance on second-hand knowledge beyond what was part of the initial stock acquired in one's youth.[39] Some people lack sufficient intelligence to understand much of what they hear. Others are out of touch with reality in varying degrees, living in private mad worlds of their own. Others though not lacking capacity still lead lives that are information poor, with drastically impoverished ideas of the world outside their immediate physical surroundings; the world ends a few blocks away from their lodgings. (Geographers have reconstructed the mental maps of the physical environment of members of different social groups, with dismaying and pathetic consequences. With extreme economic poverty is often found extreme poverty of ideas about where one is.)[40] An impoverished mental representation of the world implies an impoverished view of what there is to know about and lack of a sufficiently rich conceptual inventory to allow one to interpret and understand what one might hear or read about the world outside one's immediate locality. For that matter, a sizable proportion of the population cannot read well enough to learn much of anything by that means. Information poverty is a typical soft concept, and there is no way of saying what its incidence is; but certainly there are many for whom the world is a tiny place and the supply of second-hand knowledge a very small one.

Information poverty can be a self-selected condition freely entered into and willingly endured. Self-selected information poverty is easily understandable; there are many ways of living satisfactory but information-poor lives in very small worlds. One may live in deliberate isolation from other people, rejecting the world and ignoring the flow of mere events. One may live in the world but live only for present enjoyment, as a young person may live simply and entirely for surfing or music for a while. One may live a life of informationally self-contained work and free time devoted to activities of building and making, like wood-work and gardening, or a life of contemplation, watching the changing seasons and reflecting on the strangeness of existence. Why, after all, do we think that people should want to know more of the world than they can discover at first hand?

Think what one might say in defense of an information-poor life. "It is known to me that there are billions of other people living and suffering variously; I am content to remain ignorant of the details. What is it to me who is the new prime minister of Norway, or how the rich are struggling to increase their riches by hiring and firing politicians? It is known to me that people hold strong opinions on how the world ought to be run, on what is wrong with it and what ought to be done about it. I am content to let them squabble among themselves. I am aware that the world of learning is awash with people proposing new theories and demolishing old ones. The important facts about the universe for us are that we live for a while and then die, and I understand that well enough without needing more detailed knowledge of the changeable views of the learned. I am content with what I have; I cultivate my garden." There are things one needs to know that one must learn from others, but not a great many of them; life can be arranged so that the necessary minimum of second-hand knowledge is available when needed. Information poverty need not feel like poverty; it need not be poverty except in relation to a standard of well-informedness that one rejects. That standard is a matter of class expectation or general social expectation, but one need not accept the standard. Lives of voluntary economic poverty are familiar and respected; members of religious orders provide examples. Lives of voluntary information poverty might similarly claim respect rather than commiseration.

Most people live in cognitive worlds somewhat larger than these information-poor worlds, but perhaps not strikingly larger.[41] Consider a common pattern: a person working in an informationally self-contained job, a nonparticipant in public affairs, with elective time centered on home and family and television entertainment. This is life in a small world, a constricted space of information, a narrow psychological space. Except perhaps for sporting events seen on television, the things of interest are private and local: one's job, house, family, and friends. Books play no part in this life; newspapers are casual sources for light world watching. Past and future are hazy, and the present is primarily the immediate local present. The rest of the world is largely irrelevant. Government and political system are simply there, like the weather, to grumble about but not to think much about.[42] If religion is part of this life, it is likely to be a matter of social participation in a local institution, with few and vague ideas and no concern for doctrine, or else rigid adherence to a strictly defined authoritative creed. Questions of cognitive authority arise infrequently. At work they are settled for one; away from work they seldom arise because one has few questions of any kind, or few that cannot be settled by already established cognitive authorities (friends, pastor, family doctor). Intelligence and understanding are by no means lacking, but they are characteristically exercised on strictly local and personal matters. Suspicion and hostility are likely to be directed toward experts in general or anyone claiming knowledge in fields that are not familiar from some personal experience. "The abstract rhetoric of their more cosmopolitan superiors is distrusted. The only accurate information is about what known individuals are doing."[43]

In normal times, the majority of people fall more or less clearly into this category, both working class and much of the middle class being included here. In times of great trouble and social upheaval, the information space may enlarge rapidly; it is not necessarily so small. But in normal times, lack of interest and lack of responsibility for significant public action combine to remove the need for filling a larger information space, and so reduce actual dependence on second-hand knowledge.

For people in professional occupations with a background of higher education, the world is likely to be larger, the information space in which one lives more extensive.[44] The public world of social and political issues is likely to occupy more space as an object of attention, if not of much involvement. The world one watches is likely to involve more than the immediate locality; one's picture of the world has more past and more future to it. The profession that one practices looms large in one's picture, not as a geographically local organization but as a community distributed all over the country or the world. The world is larger but skewed by a disproportionate interest in and attention to a single area of activity and a single group of actors. And though larger, it may not otherwise differ much from smaller worlds. The product of specialization has been, one commentator writes, "a specialist who shares little of the inherited culture and whose views and tastes outside his own specialty are too often like those of a much less educated person . . . [including] a very meager and miscellaneous knowledge outside his special subject."[45] The profession itself solves the principal problems of cognitive authority, and fairly shallow involvement in and little responsibility for public issues means that authority problems arising there can be treated lightly. "We need only compare a lawyer's attitude to his brief and the same lawyer's attitude to the statements of political fact presented in his newspaper in order to see . . . that without the initiative that comes from immediate responsibility, ignorance will persist in the face of masses of information however complete and correct."[46]

Lack of responsibility permits easy solution to authority questions. And the principle of professional deference is likely to produce a readiness both to accept the views of experts and to suppose that there are solutions to problems that can be provided by experts. To the professional, the world is divided into professional provinces, and the proper organization of social life consists in assigning to each province authority over the problems it is best equipped to solve. Professionalism is a world view according to which every problem is the province of some profession or a committee of professionals. One need not concern oneself with matters that fall within the sphere of another profession, and one should not, by the rule of professional deference.

If we are right about the responsibilities of the generalist director of affairs and the cognitive consequences of those responsibilities, then the cognitive world of such a person is likely to be more extensive than that of the professional and more realistic about the relative importance of the various groups of experts. But the engaged man of affairs—whether in business, government, political action, or administration—is almost certain to substitute a different sort of exaggeration, for of course his enterprise—business, party, country, cause—looks as large in his picture of the world as does the profession in the professional's picture. And his view of the world is likely to be ruthlessly selective, cutting out whatever does not affect his enterprise. A wide-ranging but purely practical attention to the world does not guarantee a wide vision of the world. The past and most of the practically irrelevant present can be ignored. The manager in his way is also a specialist: specializing in the range of things that are likely to affect his enterprise, and ignoring all else. He is dependent more than others on second-hand knowledge and must face and solve questions of cognitive authority that others can ignore. His picture of the world, however, can be as distorted as that resulting from any other kind of specialization. Responsibility calls for a big, but does not guarantee an accurate or balanced, picture of the world.[47]

All of the sorts of people considered so far find ways of living with cognitive maps of the world that are relatively small and lacking in detail outside areas of immediate practical concern, except for optional areas filled with information gathered in the course of world watching and participation in one or more of the many cultural subworlds. But surely there are people who deliberately set themselves the goal of gaining as comprehensive as possible a picture of the world. Let us define a group by an ideal: those who belong to the group are those who accept and try to reach the ideal. The ideal is simply that of the most extensive and properly proportioned view of the world, the most comprehensive understanding of the whole of life and the world in which it is lived. It calls for a strong sense of the past, as much concern with the future as with the present, cosmopolitan rather than local concerns and interests, a view of the world free from egocentricity and from the perspectival distortions of one's particular social, geographical, and temporal location. It is the ideal of a view of the world based on the best help one can get from those most worthy of cognitive authority, making the best possible use of others' inquiries. It is, in effect, the ideal of the ultimate generalist, undertaking to put the contributions of specialists in their proper place. And it is an ideal the pursuit of which creates the greatest burdens of decision about cognitive authority, for the range of questions to which one wants the best available answer is wide open.

No one attains this ideal, not with a lifetime of trying, but people do pursue it, with varying degrees of intensity. Let us call the people who do so intellectuals, with full realization that the term intellectual is elsewhere used in a wide variety of more or less inconsistent and controversial ways.[48] Intellectuals, as we understand them, can be found anywhere in society. Being an intellectual is not an occupational specialization or the predominant or exclusive characteristic of any economic or social stratum. No doubt many are found in the academic world, but not all academics are intellectuals. Many are firmly committed to the principle of specialization and to accepting what Arthur Balfour called "the pernicious doctrine that superficial knowledge is worse than no knowledge at all."[49] An intellectual may be a specialist but as an intellectual tries to treat his specialty as no more than one small, special way of inquiring. Included in the group of intellectuals are the remnants of the old class of educated nonspecialist general readers, people of general culture, a class said now to be "if not obsolete, at least obsolescent, . . . being driven out of existence by the elimination of the leisured classes on the one hand and by the growth of specialization on the other."[50] The classification of individuals as intellectuals is a prime example of what we have called soft classification.

If the ideal by reference to which we identify the group of intellectuals imposes the greatest burdens of answering questions of cognitive authority, still the burdens may not be felt to be heavy, for pursuit of the ideal is a voluntary, self-assigned task and partakes of the character of a game. Solving problems of cognitive authority is a central part of this game, and problem solving is not burdensome if done as a central part of an activity undertaken for its own sake. Further, decisions may be as tentative as one likes and may be postponed indefinitely. If they are felt as too difficult, they may be left aside entirely. It is one's own picture, after all, and one can put in and leave out what one likes.

That is, of course, just the trouble. One is unconstrained by anything except one's comprehension of what others have to offer and one's sense of what is worth taking seriously and what can be ignored as of no importance: one's intellectual taste. To anyone actively engaged either in the attempt to work out "adequate summations, cohesive assessments, comprehensive orientations," or to evaluate critically others' attempts, the conclusions to which others come may seem so bizarre, and the play of intellectual fashion so pronounced, as to make one doubt whether the attempt is worth making at all.[51] Working only with materials at hand in one's environment, one may find little that is available for use either because, as in the case of science, one cannot understand much of it or because, as in the case of the human studies, there is little that one finds oneself able to take seriously.[52] Rather than admiring the attempts of the ambitious intellectuals to gain a very large view of the world, one may end by despairing of their ability to do other than make themselves ridiculous. It might have been thought that our sequence of sketches of successively larger information spaces could be interpreted as a sequence of successively improved pictures of the world: as if one could see more the higher one mounted on the social scale, until with the intellectual, one climbed off that scale entirely. But that would be to be misled by the metaphor of perspective discussed at the outset of this book. That large view is not one that one has or gets automatically just by detaching oneself from a small local scene and opening one's intellectual eyes. It is one that is constructed, and the large construct is not necessarily better than the small one. A construct may seem bizarre because of defects of proportion: overemphasis on this, underemphasis on that. These are by now familiar expressions of intellectual taste. It may seem based on an entirely erroneous conceptual scheme. One may think that a big picture drawn according to one of the available really grand theories—Marxism, Christian doctrine—is likely to be a poor picture of the real world. The big picture constructed under the guidance of a crude or eccentric intellectual taste may seem far more objectionable than the small pictures of those living in voluntary information poverty. It is a mistake to think that large views are generally better—more accurate or more reliable—than small ones. The less one's views are confined to what one can learn or verify at first hand, the more one depends on the authority of others, with nothing but one's intellectual taste to guide one at the end. But as anyone can verify for himself by looking around, that is not a reliable guide.

Notes

1. Warren Harding, quoted in Richard Fenno, *The President's Cabinet* (Cambridge: Harvard University Press, 1959), pp. 40-41.

2. E. Adamson Hoebel, "Authority in Primitive Societies," in *Authority*, ed. Carl J. Friedrich, Nomos 1 (Cambridge: Harvard University Press, 1958), pp. 226-27.

3. Milton Rokeach, *Beliefs, Attitudes, and Values* (San Francisco: Jossey-Bass, 1968), pp. 9-10.

4. Patrick Wilson, *Public Knowledge, Private Ignorance: Toward a Library and Information Policy* (Westport, Conn.: Greenwood Press, 1977), pp. 45-53.

5. Milton Rokeach, *The Open and Closed Mind* (New York: Basic Books, 1960), p. 45.

6. Angus Campbell et al., *The American Voter: An Abridgement* (New York: Wiley, 1964), Ch. 5, for party identification.

7. Andrew Hacker, "Farewell to the Family?" *New York Review of Books*, 18 March 1982, p. 42.

8. Ibid.

9. James S. Coleman, *The Adolescent Society* (New York: Free Press, 1961). See the review of Coleman's book by Bennett M. Berger, "Adolescence and Beyond," *Social Problems* 10 (1963): 394-400. For Berger, the adolescent's interest in "athletics, extracurricular activities, dating, popularity, cliques, cars, dances, the mass media" rather than in book learning does not make adolescents a distinct subculture; their interests reflect adult values. "If one were looking for subcultural tendencies among adolescents, one might do worse than to look at the students

who had a strong commitment to intellectual values rather than to the students who carry the very American patterns of culture that Coleman found" (p. 397). For what high schools do in the way of preparing students for adult life, see the devastating report *Perspectives on Improving Education: Project TALENT's Young Adults Look Back*, ed. John C. Flanagan, Praeger Special Studies (New York: Praeger, 1978), p. 37: "High school education in its formal aspects serves no very useful purpose for the majority of people."

10. Howard R. Bowen et al., *Investment in Learning: The Individual and Social Value of American Higher Education* (San Francisco: Jossey-Bass, 1977), p. 88: "Most studies show that 50 to 80 percent of what is learned in courses is lost within one year." Some residues do remain, and of course college has other effects on people, extensively reviewed by Bowen. See also Herbert H. Hyman, Charles R. Wright, and John Shelton Reed, *The Enduring Effects of Education* (Chicago: University of Chicago Press, 1975), p. 21: "The better educated do have wider and deeper knowledge not merely of bookish facts but also of the contemporary world, and . . . are more likely to seek out knowledge and be attuned to sources of information."

11. This is professional socialization, otherwise known as brainwashing. At all stages of schooling, the official line is that students are learning to be critical by developing powers of analysis and evaluation; but this means learning to criticize in approved ways, developing skill at a kind of analysis and evaluation the teacher thinks appropriate.

12. *Manifesto of the Communist Party*, section II; Karl Marx and Friedrich Engels, *Basic Writings on Politics and Philosophy*, ed. Lewis S. Feuer (Garden City, N.Y.: Doubleday, Anchor Books, 1959), p. 26.

13. Edward Shils, *Tradition* (Chicago: University of Chicago Press, 1981), p. 250: "Power exercises a charismatic force of its own and draws in the wake of its cultural traditions those who have been overcome by it." See also Bertrand de Jouvenel, *The Pure Theory of Politics* (Cambridge: Cambridge University Press, 1963), Ch. 3. And E. H. Gombrich, "The Logic of Vanity Fair," in *The Philosophy of Karl Popper*, ed. Paul Arthur Schillp, Library of Living Philosophers, 14 (LaSalle, Ill.: Open Court, 1974), pp. 945-51. Of course the whole of social psychology ought to be relevant here too. No doubt this emphasis on lability of belief and taste can be overdone. For a well-known warning to an analogous overemphasis on "man the acceptance-seeker," see Dennis H. Wrong, "The Oversocialized Conception of Man in Modern Sociology," *American Sociological Review* 26 (1961): 183-93. But it can be underdone too.

14. Most work skills are learned on the job. See *Perspectives on Improving Education*; Randall Collins, *The Credential Society* (New York:

Academic Press, 1979); Lester Thurow, *Generating Inequality* (New York: Basic Books, 1975); Harry Braverman, *Labor and Monopoly Capital: The Degradation of Work in the Twentieth Century* (New York: Monthly Review Press, 1974).

15. Stanley Aronowitz, *False Promises* (New York: McGraw-Hill, 1973), esp. pp. 304-19; Warren O. Hagstrom, "Traditional and Modern Forms of Scientific Teamwork," *Administrative Science Quarterly* 9 (1964), p. 254.

16. C. P. Snow, *Science and Government* (Cambridge: Harvard University Press, 1961), p. 72.

17. Henry Mintzberg, *The Nature of Managerial Work* (Englewood Cliffs, N.J.: Prentice-Hall, 1980), p. 30.

18. Ibid., p. 66: "In all but the least structured of organizations, each man below the manager is a specialist, and the manager, relatively speaking, a generalist. . . . He may not know as much about any one function as the specialist charged with it, but he is the only one to know a significant amount about all functions."

19. Dale E. Zand, *Information, Organization, and Power: Effective Management in the Knowledge Society* (New York: McGraw-Hill, 1981), p. 171: "An ill-structured situation is harrowing and bizarre because it is difficult to identify the expert advice-giver beforehand. However, there is no shortage of self-proclaimed experts; every specialist or administrator can claim to be an expert, and usually does. This dilemma is built into the ill-structured situation," which is the kind of situation the manager typically faces.

20. Howard S. Becker, "Whose Side Are We On?" *Social Problems* 14 (1967): 241.

21. Harold J. Laski, *The Limitations of the Expert*, Fabian Tract no. 235 (London: Fabian Society, 1931).

22. Abraham Kaplan, *The Conduct of Inquiry: Methodology for Behavioral Science* (San Francisco: Chandler, 1964), p. 28.

23. Joseph F. Coates, "What is a Public Policy Issue?" in *Judgment and Decision in Public Policy Formation*, ed. Kenneth R. Hammond, AAAS Selected Symposium, 1 (Boulder, Colo.: Westview Press, 1978), p. 58.

24. Sylvia Porter, "How to Choose and Use a Lawyer," *San Francisco Chronicle*, 19 October 1981, p. 60.

25. William J. Goode, "Community within a Community: The Professions," *American Sociological Review* 22 (1957): 194-200, esp. 198-200.

26. Michael L. Ray and Donald A. Dunn, "Local Consumer Information Systems for Services: The Market for Information and Its Effect on the Market," in *The Effect of Information on Consumer and Market Behavior*, ed. Andrew A. Mitchell (Chicago: American Marketing As-

sociation, 1978), p. 94. This they describe as the "information avoidance strategy."

27. Peter Steinfels, *The Neoconservatives* (New York: Simon & Schuster, 1979), p. 233, notes that the neoconservatives are correct in identifying a contemporary attack on professional authority and technical expertise; but while they see this as populist leveling and resentment against the authority represented in superior competence, Steinfels argues that hostility to professional authority is often based rather on disbelief, often backed with evidence, that the claimed competence is actually superior or even competent. The principle that superiority deserves special consideration is not at stake, he thinks.

28. See Richard Nisbett and Lee Ross, *Human Inference: Strategies and Shortcomings of Social Judgment* (Englewood Cliffs, N.J.: Prentice-Hall, 1980), pp. 45-60, on the effect of "vividness."

29. See William Stephenson, *The Play Theory of Mass Communication* (Chicago: University of Chicago Press, 1967).

30. This is rather like Herbert Gans's distinction between "expert news" and "popular news." See his *Deciding What's News: A Study of CBS Evening News, NBC Nightly News, Newsweek, and Time* (New York: Vintage Books, 1980), pp. 307-10. His *Popular Culture and High Culture: An Analysis and Evaluation of Taste* (New York: Basic Books, 1974) is relevant here as well.

The distinction between serious and light world watching is close to Machlup's distinction between "intellectual knowledge" and "small-talk and pastime knowledge"; indeed, his description of the latter category puts it almost entirely into our light world-watching category: "local gossip, news of crimes and accidents, light novels, stories, jokes, games, etc., acquired as a rule, in passive relaxation from 'serious' pursuits." Fritz Machlup, *Knowledge and Knowledge Production* (Princeton: Princeton University Press, 1980), p. 108.

31. Matthew Arnold, "The Function of Criticism at the Present Time," in his *Essays Literary and Critical*, Everyman's Library ed. (London: Dent, 1906), p. 10: "The notion of the free play of the mind upon all subjects being a pleasure in itself, being an object of desire . . . hardly enters into an Englishman's thoughts."

32. Excerpt from Ernest L. Boyer and Fred M. Hechinger, *Advancing Civic Learning* (New York: Carnegie Foundation for the Advancement of Teaching, 1981), in *Chronicle of Higher Education*, 25 November 1981, p. 12. See also Dorothy Nelkin, "Political Impact of Technical Expertise," *Social Studies of Science* 5 (1975): 35-54; Allen Mazur, "Disputes between Experts," *Minerva* 11 (April 1973): 243-62.

33. Campbell et al., *American Voter*. A widespread opinion is ex-

pressed in a graffito: "If voting changed anything, they'd make it illegal," quoted in *Mother Jones* (April 1982): 25.

34. See, for example, Robert E. Lane and David O. Sears, *Public Opinion* (Englewood Cliffs, N.J.: Prentice-Hall, 1964), Ch. 6.

35. Philip E. Converse, "The Nature of Belief Systems in Mass Publics," in *Ideology and Discontent*, ed. David Apter (New York: Free Press, 1964), pp. 206-61.

36. Leo Tolstoy, *Anna Karenina*, trans. Constance Garnett (New York: Random House, 1939), 1: 10-11.

37. The situation is quite different if I am a polemicist, actively engaged in a struggle for intellectual dominance of a position. In order to destroy what is written by the opponents, I must certainly study it. If I am on the side of creationism and am responsible for the defense of the position and the attack on the opposed position, I must be highly informed about what the other side has to say that can be used against them and for my side. Partisans who are actively engaged in intellectual struggle are often much better informed than languid supporters of the opposing position.

38. On these points see Nisbett and Ross, *Human Inference*.

39. With the five types crudely portrayed in the text, one might compare the three types in Alfred Schutz, "The Well-Informed Citizen: An Essay on the Social Distribution of Knowledge," in his *Collected Papers, II: Studies in Social Theory*, Phaenomenologica 15 (The Hague: Nijhoff, 1964), pp. 120-34: the expert, the man on the street, and the well-informed citizen.

40. Peter Gould and Rodney White, *Mental Maps* (Harmondsworth, Eng.: Penguin Books, 1974), pp. 15-49.

41. See, among an enormous number of possibilities: Joseph A. Kahl, *The American Class Structure* (New York: Rinehart, 1957); Herbert J. Gans, *The Urban Villagers: Group and Class in the Life of Italian-Americans* (New York: Free Press, 1965); Lillian Breslow Rubin, *Worlds of Pain: Life in the Working Class Family* (New York: Basic Books, 1976); Louise Kapp Howe, *Pink Collar Workers: Inside the World of Women's Work* (New York: Avon, 1978); Genevieve Knupfer, "Portrait of the Underdog," *Public Opinion Quarterly* 11 (1947): 103-14; Albert K. Cohen and Harold M. Hodges, Jr., "Characteristics of the Lower-Blue-Collar Class," *Social Problems* 10 (1963): 303-34; Benita Luckman, "The Small Life-Worlds of Modern Man," *Social Research* 37 (1970): 580-96; Thomas Childers and Joyce Post, *The Blue Collar Adult's Information Seeking Behavior and Use: Final Report* (Washington, D.C.: Educational Resources Information Center, 1976). I am assuming that the group being described here includes the working class and the part of the middle class that does not consist of profes-

sional and managerial workers. On the size of the working class, see Andrew Levison, *The Working Class Majority* (New York: Penguin Books, 1975).

42. Nigel Harris, *Beliefs in Society: The Problem of Ideology* (London: Watts, 1968), p. 56: "In times of relative social stability, a substantial proportion of the population, even a majority, is not aware of the national political arena, and does not give even what Edmund Burke called 'a sort of heavy lumpish acquiescence' to government . . . . Rather are the state and its agencies much like the weather, something one must tolerate as part of the natural order of things, not something one can 'accept' or 'reject.' "

43. Randall Collins, *Conflict Sociology: Toward an Explanatory Science* (New York: Academic Press, 1975), p. 71.

44. See Bowen et al., *Investment in Learning*; Hyman, Wright, and Reed, *The Enduring Effects of Education*.

45. Edward Shils, *The Intellectuals and the Powers, and Other Essays* (Chicago: University of Chicago Press, 1972), p. 123; cf. Harold L. Wilensky, "Mass Society and Mass Culture: Interdependence or Independence?" *American Sociological Review* 29 (1964):173-97.

A study comparing students who had spent four years in college with high school graduates who had then worked for four years found that "as manifested by their reading habits, the college students did not appear to have increased markedly in intellectual interests more than employed youth." Bowen et al., *Investment in Learning*, p. 86.

46. Joseph A. Schumpeter, *Capitalism, Socialism and Democracy*, 3d ed. (New York: Harper & Row, Harper Torchbooks, 1962), pp. 261-62. Alfred North Whitehead, *Science and the Modern World* (New York: New American Library, Mentor Books, 1948), pp. 196-97: "Each profession makes progress, but it is progress in its own groove. . . . People have lives outside their professions or their businesses. But the point is the restraint of serious thought within a groove. The remainder of life is treated superficially, with the imperfect categories of thought derived from one profession." See also W. E. Moore, "Occupational Socialization," in *Handbook of Socialization Theory and Research*, ed. David A. Goslin (Chicago: Rand McNally, 1969), p. 881, on what the French call "déformation professionelle."

47. "A lifetime spent working one's way up the greasy corporate pole is usually a narrowing experience; it leaves the typical corporate chairman little time or energy to master the social, economic, and political problems of the nation or the world, which are the meat and drink of the Establishment." Leonard Silk and Mark Silk, *The American Establishment* (New York: Avon Books, 1981), p. 227.

48. For example, Nathan Glazer, "The Role of Intellectuals," *Commentary* (February 1971): 55: "Intellectuals are people who make a living from ideas, and are in varying degrees directly influenced by ideas. Thus they live off ideas and they live for ideas." This makes intellectuals an occupational category. See also Charles Kadushin, *The American Intellectual Elite* (Boston: Little, Brown, 1974), for a description of people who do indeed live off ideas. Richard Hofstadter, in his *Anti-Intellectualism in American Life* (New York: Vintage Books, 1963) pp. 26-28, had contrasted the professional man who lives off ideas rather than for them with the intellectual who lives for (but not necessarily, though Hofstadter is not explicit, off) ideas.

Everett Carll Ladd, Jr., and Seymour Martin Lipset, *The Divided Academy: Professors and Politics* (New York: Norton, 1976), pp. 132-33: "The intellectual is one whose activities involve the creation of *new* knowledge, *new* ideas, *new* art." So a critic would not be an intellectual, but an inarticulate painter would be. This is not satisfactory.

49. Quoted in Jacques Barzun, *Science, The Glorious Entertainment* (New York: Harper & Row, 1964), p. 27.

50. C. B. A. Behrens, "Porn, Propaganda, and the Enlightenment," *New York Review of Books*, 29 September 1977, p. 33.

51. C. Wright Mills, *The Sociological Imagination* (New York: Grove Press, 1961), p. 8. For a good example of intellectual fashion, see Sherry Turkle, *Psychoanalytic Politics: Freud's French Revolution* (Cambridge: MIT Press, 1981).

52. On science, see Lionel Trilling, *Mind in the Modern World*, 1972 Jefferson Lecture in the Humanities (New York: Viking Press, 1973); and C. P. Snow, *The Two Cultures: And a Second Look*, (New York: New American Library, Mentor Books, 1963).

6 INFORMATION RETRIEVAL AND COGNITIVE AUTHORITY

The Authority of the Printed Word

Libraries are storehouses of knowledge and of much else. They house the paper products of the knowledge industry, but that does not mean that they contain a collection of works each of which presents a contribution of knowledge. From our survey of the organization of production in the knowledge industry, we have to conclude that a complete collection of the published results of work in the industry contains a very great deal of material in the form of proposals that found little or no acceptance and that it may contain a great deal of work of no value or significance whatever. If we believe in progress in knowledge, we will have to expect that many of the older products have been made obsolete by later work. And if we suspect that fashion plays a large part in determining what is produced and what is currently thought of past productions, we will have to expect that many of the older products may have gone out of fashion even though they are still valuable and usable.

If we doubt that workers in many parts of that industry are really able to settle the questions they raise, we will recognize that much of the content of the library will represent opinion, not knowledge. If we admit that the number of different perspectives from which the world can be viewed and described is endless, we shall expect that the library will contain competing, conflicting accounts of the world that cannot be incorporated into a single consistent story of the way things are. And if we recognize the existence of a cultural underground pseudo-knowledge industry catering to the superstitious and deluded, then we will expect a complete or indiscriminate library to contain much that represents neither knowledge nor reasonable opinion at all.

We did not explicitly consider whether the production of works aimed at a nonspecialist audience should be considered part of the knowledge industry, and we need not answer that question now, simply noting the fact that while most of the specialist productions of the industry never reach any audience but a specialist one, there is a flourishing industry devoted to the production of textbooks, popularizations, and works of serious or semiserious scholarship aimed at a wide audience (including much of what we have included under the general category of history), which will be found in the library and will represent as much variation in quality and credibility as will the specialist productions. A small library might contain only "the best that has been thought and said," but a large library is bound to contain much of the worst as well. All of the books, journals, newspapers, manuscripts, and films in the world's libraries are possible sources of knowledge and opinion, but they present us with the same sorts of questions of cognitive authority that their authors would if we were face to face with them. Which of the works in the library are to be taken seriously? How much weight are we to give to what the texts say? Some of them will tell us about things of which we already know a great deal, and we can test their claims directly against what we already know (or think we know). But most of them will tell us about things we do not know enough about to apply the direct test. We consult them to find what we do not already know. And so we have to approach them as we would anyone claiming special expertise: by applying indirect tests. The tests available are similar to those we would apply to any person.

The obvious basis for recognizing the cognitive authority of a text is the cognitive authority of its author. We can trust a text if it is the work of an individual or group of individuals whom we can trust. The usual considerations that would warrant recognition of a person's authority can be transferred to his work as long as the work falls within the sphere of his authority. But at once the element of time enters to distinguish the case of textual authority from that of personal authority. The basic tests of personal cognitive authority apply to a person as he is now, at the time the tests are applied: present reputation, accomplishments up to now, and so on. That he now merits recognition as an authority does not mean that he did so earlier or that he will continue to do so. If he now merits that recognition, a work he composed twenty years ago may not merit it; for one thing, he may have repudiated it himself, and if we now trust what he says on the same subject, we cannot transfer his present authority to that past work. Present authority in the person does not automatically transfer to past work. Nor does past authority of the person automatically transfer to the text giving it any present authority. That someone was an expert on a subject in 1850 does not provide warrant for taking the texts he produced then as now having any authority at all. An old reputation is not enough to establish the present authority of old texts. It is present standing that we need to determine.

Present reputation provides the strongest practical test of the cognitive authority of an old text— not just reputation among any group of contemporaries but reputation among those we recognize as having cognitive authority in the appropriate sphere. They may or may not be those now expert in the field in which the old work originated, or in some successor field into whose scope the old questions have now passed (for the geography of inquiry changes constantly, and questions migrate from one field to another). If we recognize the authority of a specialist group now claiming jurisdiction over the sphere within which the old text falls, its present reputation in that group may be decisive for us; but if we do not recognize their authority, its reputation in that group may be immaterial to us. We can rely on personal recommendation, that being just a special case of the present reputation rule. We are prepared to trust the texts that one whom we trust tells us we can trust. But what do we do when present reputation is unknown or irrelevant and we lack personal recommendations? Since the passage of time erodes authority, we may rely on a simple rule of recency: the newer the better, the older the worse. Such a simple-minded rule is sure to lead us to neglect good old works for shoddy modern ones, but no indirect test can be expected to work all the time. And if one cannot formulate and apply any more complex time-discount rule, this simple rule is better than nothing. Given no other basis than time since writing on which to decide about the cognitive authority of texts, one would not do better by using the rule "the older the better," nor would one do better by ignoring time entirely. But more complex rules for discounting for time since writing are easy to formulate: for instance, by dividing subjects into those one suspects to be progressive and those one thinks unprogressive, applying the simple rule of recency for progressive ones and ignoring time entirely or not giving it much weight in unprogressive subjects. Whether a subject is progressive may be decided by reference to institutional authority or its most important condition, present consensus. By this rule we might come to the conclusion that science is progressive and other fields of inquiry unprogressive.

Another sort of test is applicable to texts but not to people: publication history. A publishing house can acquire a kind of cognitive authority—not that the house itself knows anything, but that it is thought to be good at finding those who do and publishing their work. So publication by a house we respect constitutes a kind of almost personal recommendation. A single journal can have the same kind of authority, which transfers to the articles it publishes. Other sorts of institutional endorsement are sometimes available and used as tests of authority: sponsorship of a publication by a learned society or professional organization; use as a textbook by teachers in prominent educational institutions; publication by a governmental agency or state printer; prizes and awards given to the text or to its author for this text. Issuance of several successive editions and translations serves as indirect test of authority, counting as an extraordinary accomplishment, since for most texts the first edition is also the last. Finally, published reviews furnish a special indirect test. If the reviewer already has cognitive authority for us, his review constitutes a personal recommendation (or not). If we are given sufficient information about the reviewer, along with the review, we may be able to arrive at an estimate of his authority. If the reviewer is unknown, his judgment may mean nothing, while if he is an anti-authority, reliably wrong, his praise may be fatal to the work he reviews.

A text may acquire cognitive authority independent of the authority of its author. The tests just enumerated are applicable

to the text directly, not first to its author and then derivatively
to the text. The authority of standard dictionaries does not derive
in our eyes from that of their compilers; we do not know these
people. A standard reference work that is repeatedly revised
may be thought of as an institution in its own right. Those
responsible for its revisions may derive their reputation from
this connection rather than the work deriving its reputation by
reflection from theirs.

Finally, the test of intrinsic plausibility, always available, is
particularly important in questions of cognitive authority of texts.
A text usually has only one chance to capture our attention and
interest; reading a few words of it may be enough to discourage
us from continuing or may lure us on to reading the whole thing.
These rapid assessments are based on more than intrinsic plausibility, but that is a large element. If the sample of text we read
strikes us as nonsense, we are unlikely to continue; if it seems
eminently sensible, we may read on. Instant recognition of a
work as representing a school of thought that we flatly reject,
a style of research that we think worthless, or a theoretic commitment that we think foolish allows us to dismiss much of what
we encounter as not worth bothering with. Not that we always
reject what we see to be in conflict with our prior beliefs and
cognitive positions—there are plenty of occasions when we must
read what we find uncongenial—but we cannot avoid awareness
of a text's contents as plausible or implausible and give or withhold authority accordingly.

Application of these various external tests for cognitive authority is as frail and uncertain as are the tests applied to people.
They can be applied in various ways with different results; however applied, they guarantee nothing. But they are all one has
to go on. Or is there a further guide to estimating the cognitive
authority of texts? Do those professionally responsible for information storage and retrieval have anything further to offer
in the way of guidance?

If we go to a library to find out what is known on some matter
or what the state of opinion is on the matter, with luck or with
the help of a librarian we may find a single source that appears
to tell us what we want to know: a reference book, a treatise, a
textbook, a review of the literature. The question that can always

be asked about the single source is, Need I look further, or can I take this source as at least provisionally settling the matter? This is the familiar question of cognitive authority in only slightly different guise. If I am already convinced of the authority of the source (it is, after all, the standard work on the subject; it is, after all, the dictionary), the question is already answered, but if I am unfamiliar with the source, the question is likely to arise explicitly, if only briefly. Since there may be many other sources giving quite different stories about what is known or what the situation is with respect to the question, it would be a mark of credulity to settle for the first source that came to hand and seemed to answer the question. Caution would suggest that one needed not only to find reasons for taking the single source seriously but also for thinking that there were no other sources deserving to be taken still more seriously. This calls for information not found in the sources themselves. We cannot tell the reputation of a text or of its author by looking at the text. Even when we think we have found out something about reputation, the question remains of what weight to give it.

If we are not so lucky as to find a single source that appears to tell us what we want to know, we may have to search for a number of texts from which, collectively, we can find what we seek. Finding the right collection of texts is neither simple nor straightforward; using the texts to arrive at a satisfactory result is even less so. The most difficult situation would be that of having to consult original reports of scholarly and scientific research, for there may be only the most tenuous and indirect relation between what they say and the consensus of the specialists, if any. The question of how much weight to give to any particular specialist group's views is ever present. It would be ideal if there were someone whom we could trust who could tell us about the single sources that seem to answer our question, "You need go no further." It would be ideal if someone could tell us about multiple sources, "You can ignore this lot, and of those remaining, this one and that one are the most important, the others adding little to what they contain."

Whoever did this would be providing us with the most important sort of quality control on texts. A text can be of high or low quality in many different ways: well and clearly written but unfortunately inaccurate; imaginative and stimulating but unsound; and so on. But for one who wants to find out what is known or what is the state of some question, the chief aspect of quality is credibility: can one believe what the text says, or can one at least take it seriously? Other good or bad points about the text are of subordinate interest. The question of cognitive authority can be rephrased as one of quality control: can those professionally responsible for information storage and retrieval act as quality controllers?

Those professionals might perform a further service: to undertake to do all our work with texts for us, including formulating an appraisal of the state of the question if no single formulation already exists that they find adequate. It would be the most luxurious service if they could not only tell us which of many texts we should consult to arrive at a good understanding of the state of the question but go on to use those texts themselves to draw up a critical description of the state of the question. We will ignore this last service for the present; one who could not be trusted to act as quality controller could not be trusted to do this further service, and we must first try to settle the question of the information storage and retrieval professional's ability to control quality.

These professionals certainly include librarians, and, increasingly, people who prefer other occupational labels, such as information specialists or information scientists. Insofar as they deal with texts, one might call them all bibliographers, though many would reject that label too. We will generally speak of librarians, understanding that what we say of them applies to others doing comparable work with comparable skills and techniques.

Misinformation Systems

It is somewhat surprising that so little attention is given in the literature of information storage and retrieval and of librarianship to the quality of the information stored and retrieved.[1] One would have thought that the difference between information and misinformation would be central in any work aimed at the design and operation and improvement of anything that called itself an information system, for if that difference was not of central importance, why not call the system a misinformation system? Libraries are still mainly called libraries, but with increasing frequency they are referred to as information centers. Unless the library is centrally concerned with the quality of what it contains, it might as well also be called a misinformation center. If people use these institutions in order to find out about some matter, then they at least are interested in the difference between finding out and being misled. The sense in which we speak of books as containing information about a subject, from which we can find out about the subject, the sense in which information is a valuable commodity, worth bothering to store and retrieve and give to people who want to learn something, is a sense in which information contrasts with misinformation.[2]

No doubt it is true that people often use libraries simply to find out what different people have said on a question, but certainly they often also want to know whether what people have said can be believed. That is a question of cognitive authority. Trying to sort out the information from the misinformation in a batch of texts that discuss the question that interests me, I have to use such clues about authority as I can find. Does the information specialist or librarian not share my concern? One would think that theoretical and practical writings about information service would be full of concern for ways of determining, measuring, or estimating and then registering the quality of the texts stored and retrieved. But they are not. The question hardly arises. Occasionally someone will complain that the question of quality is being unduly neglected. The complaints go unheard, or at any rate go without effect. Writers on collection development in libraries regularly discuss the evaluation of library materials, but it is surprising how little is said about how one is to assess the quality of a work.[3] One is regularly advised to determine the authority of the author or to investigate his qualifications, but no instructions are given as to how to do this. (Nothing like the distinction between expertise and authority is to be found in the standard works.) Writers on collection development have wrestled inconclusively with the conflict between trying to provide works of high quality and also providing works that people will be interested in reading. The conflict centers on works of literature and the different appeal of works of high and popular culture rather than on nonfiction.

What happens to a work after it enters the library is not of concern to collection development; that is the business of others. But whose business, if anyone's, is it to indicate to library users the quality of the works in the library? It is not the business of those who make the library's catalogs. While it would be feasible to provide information about the quality of works along with other information in catalog records, it is not in fact done, and it is not recognized as the job of the catalog to provide evaluative information. Of course, the catalogs of most libraries reveal rather little about the contents of the libraries' collections, since the smallest unit separately listed is usually the separately published book, or the periodical publication treated as a single unit. To find journal articles or separate chapters in collections of papers, for instance, one must use a variety of other indexes. A few of these indexes are explicitly evaluative, a combination of critical review and abstracting service, but most indexes are evaluatively neutral, indicating only content. Little in the literature on indexing betrays any strong concern for the quality of the material covered. Reference librarians are heavily involved in matters of quality, but the literature of reference work is curiously free from explicit discussions of how to determine the quality of information sources or how to decide on the proper measure of cognitive authority that should be given to a source. Librarians and others professionally concerned with information storage and retrieval shy away from the question of quality.

Librarians have a standard response to proposals that part of their professional responsibility should be to provide information about the quality of the texts that they collect, describe, and make accessible. It is that evaluation of the content of texts requires expertise in the subject matter of the text evaluated, and the librarian or information specialist does not and cannot be expected to have expertise in every subject for which there are texts, or indeed to have expertise in any subject except the techniques of librarianship or information handling. Those who prepare indexes to journal literature cannot be expected to evaluate the material they index if they are not expert in the subject matter. Explicitly or implicitly accepting this standard response, the theoreticians of librarianship and information storage and retrieval spend no time discussing how quality might or should be determined and how information storage and retrieval could incorporate quality control in its basic and essential operations. The practical rule is: *caveat emptor*. The theoretical position seems to be: that practical rule is the right rule.

This response is odd but not unprecedented. Information science is then similar to communications engineering in its indifference to the quality of messages. The communications engineer is concerned with the fast and reliable transmission of signals but not with the quality of the information content carried by the signals. It is important to the engineer that the signal received be that sent but not important that the signal represent a piece of misinformation rather than information. The kind of mistake of concern is, say, the garbling or degradation of a message, certainly not the sending of the wrong message in the first place. Analogously, the information scientist is concerned with the fast and reliable retrieval of stored messages (texts) but not with the quality of the messages. It is important that the messages received be those requested, but not important to the information scientist as such that the messages represent misinformation rather than information, or incompetent inquiry rather than competent inquiry. That is for some other specialist to determine. Questions of quality fall outside the scope of information science.

If we take this line, there are significant facets of actual library and information work that seem to lie outside the scope of the theoretical study that corresponds to that work, facets that are left without systematic theoretical investigations. First, at the input state, is not quality a consideration in deciding what to add to a library or put into a retrieval system? And who then makes the decision, and on what basis if not expertise in various subject matters? Second, at the output state, librarians answer reference questions and directly give people information (unfortunately, as we know, all too often misinformation rather than information)[4] and they sometimes (or often, depending on the situation) recommend readings to their patrons and make reading lists and bibliographies directed either to their clientele in general or to individual clients. In answering questions, recommending readings, and making lists tailored for particular publics, quality is explicitly or implicitly a major concern, or certainly should be if it is not. Is it satisfactory for theory to ignore this concern?

There is a sophisticated response to these questions. It is that the information scientist is indeed concerned with quality but in the guise of subjective utility.[5] The goal of libraries and other information systems is to provide people with texts or information that they find subjectively satisfactory. Whether others would or ought to find the same texts satisfactory is another matter and outside the scope of the science and of practice as well. The point is to provide each system user the texts that that individual will be most gratified to get. Any concern with quality that did not affect subjective satisfaction would be wasted, and success at devising ways of giving people what they find most satisfactory is a solution to any problems of quality. "When all is said and done, the major task of any library is to supply those materials which the individual user will find valuable and useful. The amount of satisfaction a reader finds in a library depends directly upon the materials the librarian has available for his/her use."[6] This, from a standard work on book selection, indicates librarians' agreement with the information scientist. Collection development is a matter of prediction, not evaluation. The aim is to collect what will be found interesting and useful, and the task is simply to try to predict which texts will be found so.

This is plausible up to a point but fails to account for question answering. The reference librarian thinks that the task is to find the correct answer to a question and that he has failed if he gives an incorrect answer, whether or not the patron was satisfied. The patron would obviously agree. No one will say that it does not matter whether a question is answered correctly or not, so long as the patron thinks it has been answered correctly. No one will admit that an information service is a good one because its users go away happy even though they have been provided inaccurate information. The selection of books for a collection may aim at satisfying the patron, but the question-answering process must aim at providing information rather than misinformation.

The sophisticated response is not even satisfactory when it

comes to finding long texts for people rather than directly answering their questions. It is satisfactory when we think only of retrieval for a specialist of texts in a specialty in which he is in his own eyes a competent judge. He expects to have to judge for himself and would not be interested in others' judgments on the texts he is given. But it is not satisfactory for the person looking for texts in an area in which he is not a specialist and does not think himself independently capable of judgment. He faces the problems of cognitive authority and might be expected to be happier with a system that gave him trustworthy indications of authority than with a system that did not. The goal of achieving the greatest subjective satisfaction cannot be reached if questions of quality, and in particular questions of cognitive authority, are ignored. Whether that goal can actually be reached is unclear, but a science that refused to consider quality would appear to be resigning itself to considering only second-best solutions.

The standard response was that evaluation can be the work only of specialists in the subject matter of the texts evaluated. This is the general principle of professional monopoly on criticism: each profession claims the exclusive right to judge its own work We have seen how much or little foundation that rule has. It is not a plain truth about who is able to do what but a political claim to certain rights and freedoms: freedom from nagging external criticism, right to do work that others may find futile and worthless. Outsiders—generalists and specialists acting as generalists—have to evaluate insiders' claims, deciding where expertise warrants recognition of cognitive authority and where it does not. Of course, the specialists—all professionals even—will resist outsiders' attempts to put an independent evaluation on their work, but that is not sufficient reason for the outsiders to stop. The stock response about lack of all the necessary expertise does not settle the issue. We must press the question further.

Demand for Evaluation

The question of quality may receive little attention from librarians and other information professionals because it is not a pressing problem, and it might fail to be a pressing problem for several reasons. The chief reason would be that no one is asking

asking them for more help than is already provided. If few or no people feel the need for help in evaluation of texts or if they feel the need but do not consider it appropriate to expect the librarian to provide the needed help, then there will be no external pressure to stimulate practical and theoretical concern for problems of evaluation by librarians and their theorists.

In fact, signs of external demand are not abundant. Workers in the knowledge industry do constantly complain of the low quality of much of what is published but do not express the desire that librarians help them determine quality. It is because they themselves feel competent to judge quality that they complain, and what they complain about is not lack of help in judging quality but lack of editorial firmness. Librarians' evaluations are not found helpful because they are outsiders' evaluations, and adherents to the principle of specialist monopoly on evaluation have no interest in outsiders' evaluations.[7] What of nonspecialists? Those uninterested in reading anything or interested in reading but not in using libraries are sources of no external pressure for evaluation. Those interested in using libraries may be satisfied with a situation in which they are left free to make their own selections without interference from librarians. If their interests are in light, recreational reading, they may be indifferent to questions of cognitive authority. Their wants can be satisfied by giving them access to a relatively small collection of recent works, as in a retail bookstore. If they are students, they are likely to be looking for what has been recommended to them by teachers, who solve any problems of authority that might arise. When we exclude nonreaders, students, specialist readers, and light readers, we have excluded most of the population. The probably tiny minority left of serious general readers, of intellectuals (in the sense earlier explained), may be in want of advice on the cognitive authority of texts from time to time, but they are also likely to be those for whom solution of problems of authority is a central part of the game they are playing. In addition, they are supplied with, and are the most likely audience for, the fairly elaborate reviewing system, especially for books. Since there is always more to read than one has time or inclination for and since plenty of texts will be known by reputation or recommendation from trusted others, the serious general reader can work at the backlog of as-yet unread works of already known standing without ever getting to the point of wondering what is worth reading next. Sometimes it is claimed that large numbers of adults want more help than they get in planning and guiding their lifelong learning, but it is not clear that this actually amounts to a desire for help from librarians in determining the authority of texts.[8] All in all, it seems as if the demand for this special kind of help is lacking or at least is only latent rather than overt. And if so, this would help to explain librarians' relative indifference to the question of quality.

But supply can stimulate demand, and a service offered might turn out to be eagerly received. Have we reasons for thinking this would happen? Have we reasons for thinking there is strong latent demand? Those who think they see the society changing in the direction of a "learning society" or a knowledge society might argue that there is such a latent demand for help in evaluation. Not long ago a serious observer could forecast that "in the middle-range future, learning might become the dominant activity for the mass of Americans . . . . In future decades when high per capita income, high rates of productivity, and high proportions of leisure time combine to permit discretionary use of time and discretionary choice of activities, it seems a safe bet that Americans will devote themselves increasingly to the intellectual endeavors." Knowledge has already become the critical economic resource, and "is fast becoming the critical resource for consumers as well. If America should become a nation devoted to learning instead of to the production of goods, the national character and the character of urbanization" would change markedly.[9]

One kind of change that might have been expected would have been an increased prominence for libraries. A nation devoted to learning instead of to the production of goods might choose learning by experience over learning at second-hand through books and other typical library materials. And if it chose book learning, it might have been so wealthy that it would buy rather than borrow its books and so enlarge the market for book publishers that public libraries would not be needed to make up for the deficiencies of the commercial book-distribution system.

But a nation devoted to learning instead of to the production of goods is at least likely to want to maintain a large stock of works available as a communal resource and not insist that one be allowed to read only those books one could afford to purchase or was able to beg from the more affluent. The greater the appetite for learning and the wider the catholicity of the appetite, the greater the potential problems of choice, of recognition of cognitive authority. The greater those problems, the more important the utility of trustworthy assistance and the possible service that the librarian might render. Others might enter the field to compete in offering the same service, to be sure, but the scope for service would be there and the possibility of rendering it would be worthy of close investigation.

Are there signs that Americans are devoting themselves increasingly to intellectual endeavors and that the nation is becoming devoted to learning instead of the production of goods? Is free time increasingly devoted to serious world watching and improvement of the understanding as well as to economically motivated enlargement of skill? It is certainly not obvious that it is.[10] The category of the general reader is not obviously growing at the expense of the other categories. Public libraries are not expanding or growing more prosperous. Thus the question of librarians' ability to help on questions of cognitive authority is not becoming an increasingly practical one. Still it is a question worth asking, for perhaps the current situation of the public library would be different if in the past the question had been answered affirmatively, or perhaps the current situation is partly explicable by a negative answer.

The Authority on Authorities

An authority on authorities is one who can be trusted to tell us who else can be trusted. He need not himself be learned in the fields in which he can identify the authorities. It is enough that he has some way of telling who deserves to be taken as having cognitive authority. A universal authority on authorities would be one who could be trusted to tell us who else can be trusted, in all possible spheres; such a person would be potentially an authority on everything, for if he could identify the authorities in any sphere, he could in principle find out what they claim to know and so inform himself on any subject whatever, and subsequently inform us. He could find out literally anything. Recalling the earlier discussion of scope, sphere, and degree of authority, it is clear that such a person need not be an absolute authority, whose word we took to settle questions for us; his word might have much less weight than that. But to be recognized as one whose word carries some weight on all possible topics would certainly be noteworthy.

Can we imagine librarians or other information specialists playing such a role? At first one is inclined to smile, thinly. But let us remember that cognitive authority is a matter of degree, and put the question again. Can we imagine them being recognized as having some degree of authority in questions of who else is to be trusted in this or that matter? Then the response is not so clear. Librarians may indeed be thought by some of their customers as specially knowledgeable about the authorities in various different spheres, and they are not obviously mistaken in this belief. Librarians are in a particularly advantageous position to survey a wide field, to be at least superficially acquainted with the work of many different people, with many books, with many works evaluating and summarizing the state of knowledge in different fields. If they are specialists in matters of techniques of bibliographical work, they are perforce generalists with regard to the content of the texts they encounter in their work. But they are in advantageous positions to develop a wide familiarity with reputations, with changing currents of thought, with external signs of success and failure. Along with knowledge of the standing of individuals, they can accumulate information about the standing of particular texts: particularly classics of different fields, standard works, and the like.

This is a long way from establishing the librarian as a universal authority on authorities. However advantageously positioned, the librarian cannot be expected to accumulate information on all possible subjects. There are too many of them and too many texts and authors. The most one might claim is that the librarian is especially well situated to find out about the standing of texts and authors in any field; he can supplement what he already knows with new information that he is especially capable of finding. Searching for information is part of the librarian's occupational role. Searching for information from which to get a conclusion about the cognitive authority of texts and authors is just a special case of searching. To deserve to be recognized as to some degree an authority on authorities, you are not required to be able always to find information that would permit a conclusion of that sort. It is enough that you are often able to find relevant information—information that tends to support one or another conclusion. The librarian can often do that. He can find information about authors' education and careers, for instance, reviews and discussions of their work, and frequencies of citations to their work—all relevant information.

This begins to sound like the description of a plausible authority on authorities, but it is not yet quite that. What does the librarian do with the information gathered? He might simply give it to the customer to use as he wishes. Or he might draw a conclusion and give that to the customer, with or without the information on which the conclusion was based. If he draws no conclusions but simply gathers information for others to use, then he is not acting as one who had found out what others' claims to cognitive authority were but simply as a supplier of background information. He need have no opinion about others' claims to cognitive authority—it does not matter if he does or does not, if he does not reveal it. The point about cognitive authority is that it is trusted for substantive judgment and specific advice, not for recital of information relevant to making judgments. We want to know from an authority on authorities whom we can trust: can I trust this author, this text? If the librarian is to serve as an authority on authorities, he has to use the information he collects and arrive at a conclusion. He has got to say, "This book is not to be trusted; that one is."

The librarian has to pronounce judgment on the cognitive authority of authors and texts. But why should anyone else take these judgments seriously? If they are based not on expertise in the subject matter concerned but only on external signs and clues, then they are based on the same sorts of things that any other person ignorant of the subject matter would have to use. The librarian would not and could not claim to have any special tests for cognitive authority that were a professional secret, unavailable to others. There are no such professional secrets.[11]

Could the librarian claim to have any special ability at interpreting the external signs and weighting them properly? Could the librarian claim, for example, to know how much importance to attach to the fact that a person graduated from Harvard or Slippery Rock State College? That his book got a good review from this person and a bad one from that one? Alas, there is no reason to suppose the librarian has this unique gift. No library educator would claim the ability to give students such a gift or claim to have it himself. Indeed any such claim would be vigorously denied by his colleagues.

It looks as if the librarian has no claim to be taken as an authority on authorities after all. This means that the librarian has no special basis for evaluation of the texts he collects and retrieves for users, no basis that everyone else does not also have, no special or distinctive claim to have his own judgments taken seriously. He can do what everyone else can do, but everyone else can do what he can do, and his judgments have no special claim of superiority. He might as well confine himself to supplying the information about authors and texts and keep his judgments to himself, which is what he would probably prefer to do anyway.

There is another route to the same conclusion, which we ought to take, for the conclusion is so important that it deserves to be treated carefully. External signs do not provide our only tests for authority; the test of intrinsic plausibility is also available and is powerful. But it is a test that obviously yields different results for different people. What I find persuasive and reasonable, you find unconvincing and foolish. A cognitive authority on authorities has to be a good judge of intrinsic plausibility. How and where would the librarian acquire this ability? Why suppose that while learning to be a librarian, one also comes to be a good judge of plausibility? There is no reason to suppose that, and no one is likely to claim that librarians are especially good at that sort of judgment. If anything, the librarian is likely to consider his own judgments of plausibility irrelevant and try to suppress subjective judgment, sticking instead to the public facts. But if he succeeds in this effort, he can make nothing of the public facts. One can arrive at no conclusions about authority solely from the facts about external reputation, education, career, and the like. One needs a way of determining how much importance to give to the facts. We all do this intuitively; without having an explicit procedure, we make subjective judgments on the relative importance of public facts. The librarian trying to suppress intuition and judgment would have to draw up an explicit scheme of weighting and grading—one scheme out of an infinity of possibilities, among which he would have no basis for choice, if determined to suppress intuition and judgment and to avoid the test of intrinsic plausibility. If he uses his intuition, he can claim no special authority; if he does not use it, he can make no claims at all. So he cannot claim authority about authorities.

That settles that, but unfortunately it also raises a serious problem. How can the librarian claim the ability to answer reference questions if he is no authority on authorities? Questions are answered in libraries by consulting books, and if the librarian cannot tell which books can be trusted and which cannot, how can he claim to have found the answer to a question?[12] He finds an answer to the question, but finding it to be the answer requires being in a position to say: "We need go no further; we may stop right here." If he cannot evaluate the cognitive authority of texts, how can he be in a position to say any such thing? This is serious; librarians cannot simultaneously deny competence to judge the quality of texts and assert competence to answer questions by finding the answers in books. Library reference service appears to be based on a contradiction: the simultaneous assertion and denial of competence to evaluate texts.

Librarians as Delegates

If a librarian cannot evaluate the content of a book, how can he tell whether the answer to a question that he finds in the book is correct or incorrect? He cannot. The librarian does, however, recognize the cognitive authority of a great many books: reference works—dictionaries, encyclopedias, handbooks, gazetteers. He recognizes their authority because it is accepted in the profession that they are to be consulted and trusted. The basis for authority is external: recommendations from other professionals, library educators, reviewers, and compilers of lists of standard reference works. Most important perhaps is the fact that the practice of reliance on such works is established. A profession is, we said earlier, a cognitive routine, and an important part of the cognitive routine of librarianship is the principle that what the profession recognizes as a standard reference work can be accepted as having cognitive authority and relied on in answering questions. The individual librarian does not have to evaluate the books from which he takes answers to questions. Others have done that already; the profession as a group has collectively decided that they can be relied on.

The particular importance of reference works in the library question-answering process lies in this: it is part of the profession's recognized business to evaluate reference works but not to evaluate other kinds of texts. The questions most readily accepted by the librarian are those of the sort answered in reference works; any particular question may happen not to be answerable from a reference work and so entail search in other sorts of texts. But a reference question is preeminently the sort of question to which a short answer can be expected to be found in a standard reference work. Other sorts of questions are likely to require long answers, for which one is directed to catalogs of books, or to be disputed or controversial or open questions, to which a single standard answer cannot be expected. Questions of opinion, open questions, are not suitable reference questions, for answers would require evaluation of sources or settling questions of cognitive authority, which the librarian does not claim to be able to do. Library question answering tries to confine itself to matters of knowledge as opposed to matters of opinion: to questions that can be assumed to be closed, with received answers recorded in reference books authorized by the profession for use. Reliance on standard reference works might be expressed this way: "For practical purposes of question answering, we will assume that the contents of these reference works reflect what we can take to be the agreed answers to questions now closed." The questions that library reference service is best prepared to answer are factual questions; but factual simply means matters of knowledge rather than opinion, closed rather than open questions—questions on which there is no controversy. That the reference works do not collectively give a single standard answer for the same question, that they are in varying degrees full of inaccuracies, that the questions they answer are often not closed but wide open: these are matters that can be admitted while still ignored in practice or ignored as long as possible. If one could not in general rely on the reference works, reference service would be impossible. If one had to answer each question by trying independently to establish the accuracy of the information given in standard reference works, the cost in time and effort would be intolerable, and unanswerable questions of cognitive authority would be encountered constantly. Reliance on the reference works taken as authoritative on the word of others is the only practical basis of reference work. The librarian can consistently deny the ability to evaluate and claim the ability to answer questions; the questions are answered on the basis of works whose authority is accepted on quite external grounds of professional standing.

If the librarian is an acceptable information source, it is not because he himself knows anything about the world outside the library and not because he is particularly good at finding out about such matters by making expert use of things inside the library. What he knows is the social standing of certain reference works within a community, the professional community of librarians, and he accepts this social standing as sufficient justification for reliance on the reference works. For the outsider, this implies that the librarian does nothing distinctive, nothing the outsider could not have done had he been supplied with similar information about the social standing of particular reference books. The question is whether that social standing is good enough to warrant recognizing the cognitive authority of the sources used to answer questions.

There is an answer that puts the work of the reference librarian in a slightly different light. Librarians as a group have no special ability to decide what texts deserve what cognitive authority, but they are no worse than many other groups in this regard. We can consciously and deliberately delegate to another person a job we could do ourselves as well as he could because we lack the time to do it or prefer not to bother doing it ourselves, and think the delegate can be trusted to do it well enough. This is the attitude we may take toward those we elect to political office.

It is not that they are better than we would be at making decisions that involve weighing the merits of competing specialists' claims but that they are no worse, and we are willing to trust them (for a while) to act on our behalf. It would be understandable that we should be prepared to make librarians our delegates as well. It is not that they are better than we would be in determining what sources of information can be trusted but that they are no worse, and we are willing to trust them to act on our behalf. They may make mistakes, but so might we. Their familiarity with the range of available sources gives them an advantage of speed in finding sources that are candidates for trust. The saving in time is sufficient inducement to appoint them our delegates, given that we think the question unimportant enough so that it can be entrusted to someone no better than ourselves, or easy enough (looking up an address or telephone number in a directory) that it would take a positive effort to fail.

This may not be very comforting to librarians, who would like to think themselves professionals with special skills at finding information. But if the special skills do not include evaluating claims to cognitive authority, it is not clear why we should recognize them as able to find information at all, except in the sense of finding out what is said in various texts. Would we really say that an individual has found out for us what the population of China is if what he does is tell us: "It says in this text that the population of China is such and such, but I have no special way of telling whether this source is to be believed or not"? Is he really an information source if he cannot tell the difference between information and misinformation? And how can he do that if he cannot evaluate the cognitive authority of the texts he uses? We would do better to say that the librarian has special skills at finding out what has been said on various questions and is perhaps no worse than we are at judging the authority of the sources.

One does not choose as one's delegate a person whose opinions and judgment seem bizarre or abnormal. The safest delegate is someone whose views are, by one's own standards, quite conventional and normal. The delegate need be no better than oneself but should at least be sensible. A person whose own views are thoroughly conventional will want as delegates people whose views are also conventional. A person whose own views are heterodox will distrust one of conventional views and prefer a delegate whose views are heterodox in the ways his own are, for those are the views that make sense to him. A delegate may serve quite successfully with no views at all, provided that he can identify the views of those for whom he serves as delegate and act as if he agreed. A chameleon might do very well as delegate.

Might not the librarian acquire a special status as cognitive authority by acquiring specialized knowledge of some subject matters—for example, by acquiring graduate degrees in economics, anthropology, history, or biology? If education as a librarian is insufficient to convince others that one is competent to evaluate the documents one stores and retrieves, would not education in something else as well be sufficient to guarantee one's competence to evaluate at least part of those documents? It should be evident that this is neither necessary nor sufficient. Not necessary, for over time one might acquire the sort of credit with a particular library user that any critic of anything might acquire, from repeated steerings of the user toward what he found rewarding. The librarian might finally come to be so trusted that when he said, "You ought to look at this," this would be taken seriously. In this sense, a librarian can gain the privilege of prescribing documents for the user. But this is a kind of authority that is acquired individually and over time, not automatically by guarantee of an institution or a pattern of training. Special training is not sufficient, particularly in areas outside the natural and formal sciences, because cognitive authority will depend on whether it is the right sort of training. Training in neoclassical economics will not confer special status for an audience of Marxists, nor training in classical Freudian psychology for an audience of behaviorists or cognitive psychologists. In areas of factional dispute, only the right sort of training will be an asset.

Librarians can individually acquire cognitive authority for particular patrons, but librarians as a group can claim no special authority. They can find out what has been said by different people on a question and can find information helpful in estimating the social standing of people and ideas and theories, information relevant to settling questions of cognitive authority. But they can claim no special competence at settling those questions. The librarian who deliberately and conscientiously tried to suppress intuition and not intrude his own notions of what is and is not plausible into the process of establishing cognitive authority would resemble the completely open-minded person who is popularly thought to be an ideal judge of such matters. But the open mind in this kind of case is the empty mind which has no reason to think one thing rather than another. We solve questions of cognitive authority by employing our already formed stocks of beliefs and preferences. If we did not do so, we could never know what to think of anything said or read.

The Didactic Library

So far we have ignored a special sort of library in which questions of cognitive authority are not only central but are answered in a special way. People uninformed about library management sometimes suppose that the presence of a book in a library constitutes an endorsement or guarantee of the book's contents. They ascribe cognitive authority to the library itself insofar as they suppose the institution is good at distinguishing good books from bad ones, or trustworthy ones from untrustworthy ones. When they find books they consider doctrinally or morally objectionable in the library, they are understandably shocked that a public agency should give its endorsement to such works and may try to get the endorsement withdrawn and the book removed from the collection. It may be difficult to convince them that the presence of the book in the collection does not constitute an endorsement, that the institution is not claiming cognitive authority. For it is, after all, feasible to form a library that claims institutional authority and tries to include only trustworthy and authoritative works.

A religious institution might include in its library only works that were doctrinally sound and considered to merit cognitive authority, or it might also include unsound or heretical works but label them as such. So might a political institution limit its library to works of proper doctrinal content. So might any professional school's library be limited to works acceptable to the profession or to the theoretical school or faction followed in the institutional program. Not only might there be such libraries; there are plenty of them. The proper office of such libraries is to serve as teaching institutions, supplying only such works as are thought fit to recommend.

An official library might be limited to works endorsed by a public governmental agency as containing only what the agency certified as trustworthy material. A library for the use of school-children might be deliberately limited to works certified by school officials as correct, trustworthy, and proper for consultation by children. All such libraries can be called didactic libraries. Presence of a book in the collection is intended to constitute an endorsement, except for books not endorsed that are clearly identified as such.[13] Such a didactic library need not contain only works that hew closely to a single doctrinal line. There can be much disagreement and many different points of view reflected in the approved works. But the disagreements and differences of point of view are those recognized as legitimate by the institution. They reflect differences of opinion within the responsible group, the tolerable divergences of opinion as well as the group consensus.

The role of the librarian in the didactic library is to anticipate or follow the judgment of the group or institution to which the library is an adjunct, not independently to determine the doctrinal soundness of particular works. The librarian might indeed evaluate particular works, acting as delegate for the institution's administrative authorities, applying standards and criteria known to be thought proper by those authorities. These might be the librarian's own internalized standards and criteria, and the librarian might do the work perfectly by following his own conscience. Or they might be standards and criteria he privately thought silly but applied as instructed, recognizing the administrative authority's right to define the working assumptions of the library. In either case, the librarian can be taken by others as having cognitive authority, being a source of information for them about the standing of particular texts. Behind the librarian lies the institution which he serves, and those who recognize the institution as itself having cognitive authority can presume that, like other educational institutions, it has ways of telling that its librarian can be trusted. The cognitive authority that the librarian would not otherwise be able to claim can be attained by reflection from that of an authoritative institution; the librarian's own soundness is warranted by the continued implied approval of the institution.

The Liberal Library

"An old dictum has it that the librarian should, *qua* librarian, have no politics, no religion, and no morals."[14] That hardly applies to the librarian of a didactic library who must have, or pretend to have, the right kind of politics or religion or morals. But it does apply to the librarian of what we can call the liberal library, in which the librarian explicitly disavows the intention to exclude works he thinks lack cognitive authority. In such a library, the librarian not only has no politics, no religion, and no morals; he has no opinion on any open question. Librarians see their role as one of complete hospitality to all opinion. "Libraries should provide books and other materials presenting all points of view concerning the problems and issues of our times," and nothing is to be done by labeling or physical segregation to "pre-dispose readers against . . . materials."[15] Answers will be gladly given to presumably factual questions (presumably closed questions) but materials, not answers, will be supplied from which the library user can find his own answer to open questions.

No library can acquire everything published, so choice is necessary, and questions of value can enter into selection decisions mainly by way of trying to determine the expertise (not the authority) of authors. But demand, not cognitive authority, is the overriding consideration, and even the productions of the information underworld are to be supplied if they are wanted. It is not to count against a text that the librarian, or a majority of people, or a vocal minority of people, find the views expressed in a text to be ridiculous or intolerable or just mistaken, and so unworthy of serious attention. It is a point of principle and pride that the librarian does nothing to influence readers for or against any view. The librarian takes it as a high principle to maintain a studied neutrality; the librarian is professionally noncommittal.

This is an ideal, not necessarily realized in practice. In practice the librarian may discretely avoid arousing controversy by setting limits to what can be collected, avoiding material that is blatantly offensive to large groups of people or to vocal small groups. In practice, the liberal library may not be completely liberal, but it has at any rate a clear and simple principle: prefer one book over another to the extent that the first is more likely than the second to be found satisfactory by a user of the library. The contrast between didactic and liberal could hardly be more extreme. In the one, cognitive authority is the dominant consideration; in the other, consumer demand is the dominant consideration.

Not only collection development principles are different in the two sorts of libraries. The scope and character of reference work should be expected to differ. In a certain sense, more is known in the didactic library than in the liberal library. The didactic library represents a group with a definite position, and there may be a large range of questions that are settled within that group, though they may be unsettled in the larger world. The public librarian cannot answer a question about theological matters, for theology is a matter of opinion; but it is not a matter of opinion inside a religious community, and for the didactic librarian it may be easy to answer questions that the liberal librarian cannot answer. The liberal librarian can discover what answers different groups might give to an open question (open in the larger community), but this is hardly the same as discovering the answer. That, the didactic librarian may well do; of course, librarians in opposing didactic libraries will give different answers. The liberal librarian knows less than the didactic librarian because the range of things that everyone thinks to be closed is much smaller than the range of things that various subgroups think closed.

The Skeptical Librarian

At the beginning of this chapter, we introduced and then put aside the possibility that the information storage and retrieval professional might not only serve as quality controller, a trustworthy guide to the cognitive authority of texts, but might also use the texts to make an appraisal or appreciation of the state of a particular question if none already existed that was satisfactory. We have fairly well disposed of that service. If the librarian can make no claim to special ability to evaluate the cognitive authority of texts, he can surely make no claim to special ability to appraise a cognitive situation. He might indeed summarize what has been said on a question and find information from which one might conclude what, for instance, were minority views and what were majority views. Acting as delegate, he might make an appraisal that was unpretentiously simply his own reaction. But he would claim no special status as critic. Since there are plenty of people claiming special status as critic, it is unsurprising that work of this sort has not become a recognized part of the librarian's customary repertoire.

It would have been interesting if the librarian's job had come to be that of gatekeeper of last resort, determining what should and should not be published. That was the job proposed for the librarian by the Spanish philosopher Ortega y Gasset. Librarians were to be responsible for preventing publication of superfluous books and encouraging production of those that are needed but not so far produced.[16] It is not clear why he thought that anyone would be prepared to give this job to librarians. Somewhat more modestly, it might have become the job of librarians or bibliographers to screen publications and weed out the futile and useless ones, omitting them from bibliographies and library collections and computerized bibliographical data bases. It has not come to be agreed that this is for the librarians and bibliographers to do. The historian of science George Sarton was well aware of the crowds of "infinitesimal and immature publications" that crowd libraries and bibliographies, but he concluded that none could be discarded entirely, and that "we are doomed to drag them along in our bibliographies, forever and ever."[17]

So the librarian and the bibliographer work in a world of texts that they take as simply given and cannot on their own authority claim to evaluate. They can claim to be especially adept at locating particular inhabitants of that world and at reporting what they say about each other and about the external world. This is a sufficiently useful and interesting skill, so librarians need feel no embarrassment at not also being independently authoritative universal authorities on authorities. The librarian's sphere concerns questions about who has said what about what and where it has been said—a large enough area for interesting and useful work.

But it is understandable by now that so little attention should be given in the literature of information science and librarianship to questions of quality. Insofar as that literature addresses practical questions, it is concerned with how the librarian or bibliographer might change what they do. Even the most abstract and formal investigation of information storage and retrieval is aimed at discovering ways in which librarians might alter their procedures or ways in which machines might do better or faster (or both) what librarians do. If the librarian's tasks include the application of standards of evaluation of cognitive authority, as in the didactic library or bibliography, the standards are given from the outside. Choice of standards is not a problem, hence not in need of solution; or if it is a problem, it is not for the librarian to decide. If what they do involves not the application of standards of evaluation but simply prediction of future reactions by users of library or bibliographical systems, again evaluation is not a problem and hence not in need of solution. If the librarian could on his own authority adopt a new set of standards of evaluation, there would be scope for inquiry into what standards ought to be adopted. But on that point there are as many people claiming competence to provide the answer as there are those who say they know how to conduct inquiry and evaluate results. It would be a hopeless task to compete with literally everybody else in the knowledge industry in an attempt to be recognized as the authorities on standards of evaluation in general. Thus evaluation falls out as a problem of no interest— because evaluation is not the aim, because the standards are supplied by others, or because there is no hope of doing anything to change standards of evaluation over the opposition of others, and no need to change them if they are already approved by others.

The liberal librarian's studied neutrality on all open questions can be and is argued for on grounds of intellectual freedom and opposition to censorship. It is right to avoid taking positions on open questions; it would be wrong to do so. Since this implies that it is wrong to be a didactic librarian, the liberal librarian is in the illiberal position of taking a position on the open question whether all libraries should be liberal rather than didactic. It is not a comfortable position to defend. Perhaps it can be understood simply as making a virtue of necessity. Since the liberal librarian can make no claim for cognitive authority on questions of the value of texts, he declares that it would be a violation of professional obligations to do so even if he could.

There is, however, a radically different way of viewing that studied neutrality. The liberal librarian can be viewed as a professional skeptic about claims to knowledge or claims of the superiority of one opinion over another. Skepticism is an ancient and seemingly indestructible current of thought, much misunderstood and maligned. Two main brands of skepticism are identifiable in the ancient world: academic skepticism, which denied the possibility of knowledge, and Pyrrhonian skepticism, the attitude of one who neither asserted nor denied the possibility of knowledge but continued to inquire, though always unsatisfied that knowledge had yet been found.[18] Noting the existence of counterarguments for every argument, noting the varying, changing character of opinions, the skeptic would simply refrain from declaring for or against any particular claim to know about the world. "Philosophical skeptics have been engaged in inquiry into alleged human achievements in different fields to see if any knowledge has been or could be gained by them," as one expert (authority?) in the subject puts it.[19] Pyrrhonian skeptics would not conclude that nothing could be gained by inquiry of some sort but rather would find themselves unconvinced that anything had been established so far. Pyrrhonism is not a doctrine but a state of mind.

Let us try to imagine how a Pyrrhonian skeptic who found himself at a library reference desk and was asked some question would answer: "As to that question, there appear to be two different opinions held by various people. I take no position on the matter myself, but I can tell you what appears to be said on each side of the question, and on each side against the other side. Of course, you are not interested in what just anyone says; you want to know who is worth listening to. As to that question, I take no position myself, but I can tell you what people say about who is worth listening to. Of course, you are not interested in what just anyone says about who is worth listening to. You want to know whose opinions on that question are worth taking seriously. I take no position on that matter, though I can tell you who the different people are and what they say about why they should be attended to. If you want more than that, I can tell you only what people say. You want a guarantee or at least a recommendation from me, but I give no guarantees and make no recommendations. You fear that if you believe this one rather than that, you may be misplacing your trust. As to that, it appears to me that you may well be right."

Does not this skeptical response closely resemble the liberal librarian's response to an open question? And would it not do perfectly well even for what the librarian thought closed questions? For the librarian need take no position on whether the questions are really closed. All he need do is report which people appear to think they are closed and what they take to be the answer. The librarian's distinction between answerable and unanswerable questions can be construed as the distinction not between matters of fact or knowledge and matters of opinion but between matters on which there appears to be no difference of opinion and those on which there does appear to be such a difference. The skeptic's intellectual position is the liberal librarian's official and professional position. Although it may be usual to consider the library profession's commitment to intellectual freedom and opposition to censorship as its main ideology, it would seem better to take Pyrrhonian skepticism as the official ideology of librarianship. In private life the librarian may be as dogmatic or credulous as anyone else, but in public life he acts like a skeptic. (Conversely, the didactic librarian who acts like a dogmatist may actually be a skeptic, appearing in public as a dogmatist.) Contrary to perpetual misunderstanding, the skeptic is not debarred from action or work; the one thing he does not do is to take a position as to whether what appears to be so really is. "It appears that this is what these people think on the question. As to whether they do really think that, I take no position," he says. One might argue (this book is in effect such an argument) that skepticism is a highly appropriate attitude to take toward the productions of the knowledge industry. Opinions may differ sharply over whether that industry produces much of value. We may, like the world watcher, be absorbed in watching the play of opinion, and help others make their way through the jungle of the bibliographical world to find what people have to say on various questions, without feeling inclined or required to take a position on the cognitive value of what we find there. We may well learn what they have to say, but for us it remains just that—what they say. Skeptic, world watcher, librarian: all take the same attitude toward the world of ideas.

Notes

1. Less attention, surely, than is given to the question by other students of information systems. See, for example, Russell L. Ackoff, "Management Misinformation Systems," *Management Science* 14 (December 1967): B147-56. It is not that nothing is ever said in information science journals about quality; rather, what little is said takes the form of editorial complaints that little is said.

2. See Fred I. Dretske, *Knowledge and the Flow of Information* (Cambridge: MIT Press, 1981), pp. 40-47. "Roughly speaking, information is that commodity capable of yielding knowledge, and what information a signal carries is what we can learn from it" (p. 44). Knowledge is something people have; information is something messages carry. Being a philosopher, Dretske requires truth in information as much as in knowledge. False information is not a kind of information at all. We can substitute "what we can take as being true" for "true": wanting information rather than misinformation is wanting what one can take as true.

3. See Wallace John Bonk and Rose Mary Magrill, *Building Library Collections*, 5th ed. (Metuchen, N.J.: Scarecrow Press, 1979); Robert N. Broadus, *Selecting Materials for Libraries* (New York: H. W. Wilson Co., 1973); William A. Katz, *Collection Development: The Selection of Materials for Libraries* (New York: Holt, Rinehart and Winston, 1980).

4. See, for example, Terence Crowley and Thomas Childers, *Information Service in Public Libraries: Two Studies* (Metuchen, N.J.: Scarecrow, 1971).

5. See W. S. Cooper and M. E. Maron, "Foundations of Probabilistic and Utility-Theoretic Indexing," *Journal of the Association for Computing Machinery* 25 (1978): 67-80; W. S. Cooper, "On Selecting a Measure of Retrieval Effectiveness," *Journal of the American Society for Information Science* 24 (1973): 87-100, 413-24.

6. Bonk and Magrill, *Building Library Collections*, p. 1.

7. A comment on the *Serials Review* by an English professor: "It is still aimed primarily at librarians, and reflects their biases. So far, it doesn't seem to be as useful for those of us in other fields." Karen J.

Winkler, "When It Comes to Journals, Is More Really Better?", *Chronicle of Higher Education*, 14 April 1982, p. 22.

8. K. Patricia Cross, *The Missing Link: Connecting Adult Learners to Learning Resources* (New York: College Entrance Examination Board, 1978), p. 9.

9. Melvin M. Webber, "Urbanization and Communications," in *Communication Technology and Social Policy*, ed. George Gerbner et al. (New York: Wiley, 1973), pp. 293-94.

10. Most of the large numbers of adults enrolled in adult-education courses are pursuing vocational goals: taking courses to prepare themselves for better jobs or, in the case of schoolteachers, to qualify for salary increases. See the distribution of registrations in noncredit courses by subject matter in "Fact File: Adult-Education Students, Number of Registrations in Noncredit Courses, 1979-80," *Chronicle of Higher Education*, 4 November 1981, p. 12.

11. Certainly there are no hints in the textbooks cited in note 3 that librarians know more than the textbooks are telling.

12. A wonderful remark in Margaret Hutchins, *Introduction to Reference Work* (Chicago: American Library Association, 1944), p. 37: "One other puzzling problem in *some* questions is ascertaining that a right answer has been found" (my emphasis). Cf. Patrick Wilson, *Public Knowledge, Private Ignorance: Toward a Library and Information Policy* (Westport, Conn.: Greenwood Press, 1977), pp. 99-107.

13. There is a strong analogy between the didactic-versus-liberal contrast and the traditionalist-liberal contrast in book selection drawn by William Katz (*Collection Development*, p. 89); also between Gans's supplier and user orientations: see Herbert J. Gans, "Supplier-Oriented and User-Oriented Planning for the Public Library," in his *People and Plans* (New York: Basic Books, 1968), pp. 95-107.

14. Broadus, *Selecting Materials for Libraries*, p. 25.

15. *Library Bill of Rights*, adopted June 18, 1949, amended February 2, 1961, and June 27, 1967, by the American Library Association Council; *Statement on Labeling, An Interpretation of the Library Bill of Rights*, Adopted July 13, 1951, Amended June 25, 1971, by the American Library Association Council.

16. José Ortega y Gasset, "The Mission of the Librarian," *Antioch Review* 21 (1961): 133-54. As the sociologist William J. Goode says, the librarian is a gatekeeper who cannot keep anyone out; see his "The Librarian: From Occupation to Profession," *ALA Bulletin* 61 (May 1967), 544-55.

17. George Sarton, "Synthetic Bibliography, with Special Reference to the History of Science," *Isis* 3 (1921): 161.

18. Arne Naess, *Scepticism*, International Library of Philosophy and Scientific Method (London: Routledge & Kegan Paul, 1968); Sextus Empiricus, *Outlines of Pyrrhonism*, with an English translation by R. G. Bury, Loeb Classical Library (London: Heinemann, 1935).

19. Richard H. Popkin, "Skepticism," *Encyclopedia of Philosophy* (New York: Macmillan, 1967), 7:449.

BIBLIOGRAPHICAL ESSAY

Readers will understand why I am not going to provide an authoritative list of references to works on cognitive authority and related topics. The works that I have found most helpful appear in the chapter notes. A list of further readings that someone else might find helpful would be either endless or arbitrarily selected. But the general bibliographical situation facing anyone interested in the topics of this work deserves some comment. Two features stand out: the lack of books of comparable scope and the extreme scatter of relevant material.

Where are the other books on cognitive authority? To one immersed in the topic, it seems of such centrality to an understanding of the human situation that one would have thought that whole libraries would have been written on it. It is distinctly surprising to find that the most nearly comparable work was published in 1849, with a second edition in 1875. Although thousands of books deal in passing with the topic and more thousands deal extensively with parts of the subject matter of this book, only in Sir George Cornewall Lewis's *An Essay on the Influence of Authority in Matters of Opinion* (London: J. W. Parker, 1849; 2d ed., London: Longmans, Green, 1875) is cognitive authority the explicit focus of an entire extensive work. (I should say, more carefully, that Lewis's work is the only one I have found. The bibliographer's nightmare, of the perfectly relevant book undiscovered after patient search, suggests caution, and I have not systematically searched for works in all languages.) Lewis does not use the phrase *cognitive authority*, to be sure, but his topic is my topic. He is concerned, as I am not, with defining the proper limits of authority, especially in religion and government, and there is certainly no point-for-point correspondence between his subtopics and mine. Still it is the nearest book.

Despite two editions, Lewis's book had no great influence. Harold Laski wrote to Justice Oliver Wendell Holmes, Jr., in 1923 that he had read the book, "which quite justified [Walter] Bagehot's remark that if you didn't know anything about a subject, George Lewis has proved that you ought to ask someone who did" (*Holmes-Laski Letters*, ed. Mark DeWolfe Howe [Cambridge: Harvard University Press, 1953], p. 539).

Bagehot actually had said that Lewis's book was so described by "a hasty thinker," which is a different matter. Bagehot thought that it would have been a good book if Lewis had not been so systematic. The acute observations and interesting examples were so heavily larded with unnecessary and already familiar detail that "the reader yawns and forgets" (Walter Bagehot, *Works*, ed. Forrest Morgan [Hartford, Conn.: Travelers Insurance Co., 1891], 3: 255). Bagehot is, unfortunately, correct. But Lewis's tendency to overlay his writings with what Bagehot called "superfluous erudition" (*Works*, 3: 234) makes his book a valuable bibliographical guide to previous writings on the topics he discusses with such relentless thoroughness.

How can one account for the apparent lack of scholarly interest in such a topic? Epistemology, the theory of knowledge, has been perhaps the central concern of philosophy, particularly since the time of Kant, and the topic of cognitive authority would seem to fall clearly within the scope of epistemology. But philosophers have been interested primarily in first-hand knowledge, to such an extent that a modern philosopher, turning to the question of the evidence of testimony in a treatise on belief, could say (as noted before: chapter 2, note 1) that there were no standard views on the topic, unlike the other major questions of epistemology. The bibliography of philosophical writings on authority (chapter 2, note 1) is strikingly barren of extended treatments of the question. Certainly one finds discussions of the topic scattered through the writings of the major philosophers (for example, Locke's discussions of probability and of "wrong assent" in book IV of his *Essay Concerning Human Understanding* [London 1690]). But the topic has not been a central one, being completely overshadowed by the question of first-hand knowledge.

The other field in which one would expect to find the topic treated is the sociology of knowledge. There, too, it has been generally neglected (but see James T. Borhek and Richard F. Curtis, *A Sociology of Belief* [New York: Wiley, 1975]). The sociology of knowledge has had difficulty in shaking off a concern for philosophical problems, in becoming a social epistemology independent of philosophical epistemology. A sociologist notes about graduate students in the sociology of knowledge that "it is ontology and epistemology they wish to discuss, not sociology" (Bernard Barber, "Toward a New View of the Sociology of Knowledge," in *The Idea of Social Structure: Papers in Honor of Robert K. Merton*, ed. Lewis A. Coser [New York: Harcourt Brace Jovanovich, 1975], p. 104). As long as the sociology of knowledge looked toward philosophy, it might have been expected to slight topics of no interest to philosophers. That situation is now changing.

If cognitive authority has not been the explicit focus of much work, still almost everybody is likely to have something to say on the topic or on near relatives of the topic, and a large number of specialties, particularly in the social sciences and in psychology, produce work strongly relevant to the topic. Both old and new work in the psychology of belief contribute something to the topic: see the works of Rokeach and Bem noted in chapters 2 (note 5) and 5 (notes 3, 5). The psychology of religious belief in particular provides pertinent material (though not much progress has been made since William James wrote *The Varieties of Religious Experience* (New York: Longmans, Green, 1902) and *The Will to Believe* (New York: Longmans, Green, 1897). There is no sharp line between change of belief and change of attitude, and so the voluminous literature of social psychology on attitude formation and change should be relevant. The results of that work are, however, ambiguous and disappointing. For a review, see William J. McGuire's chapter in the *Handbook of Social Psychology,* 2d ed. (Reading, Mass.: Addison-Wesley, 1969), 3: 136-314. The topic of intellectual fashion gets little attention in the general literature on fashion, which is treated in sociology and social psychology as just one aspect of collective behavior. Fashion is, of course, of interest in such fields as home economics and marketing. A good bibliography, not confined to questions of dress, is found in George B. Sproles, *Fashion: Consumer Behavior toward Dress* (Minneapolis: Burgess Pub. Co., 1979), pp. 219-36. The relevant material for other topics treated in chapters 3 and 4 is almost overwhelming, including much of the sociology of science (currently a lively field), some (but not much) of the philosophy of science and the philosophy of the social sciences in particular, and a large but extremely scattered quantity of critical, self-critical, apologetical, and controversial literature on the status of the various disciplines. For the question of cognitive authority in everyday life, the sociology of work and of the professions provides relevant material, as does the study of the process of socialization (see the *Handbook of Socialization Theory and Research,* ed. David A. Goslin [Chicago: Rand McNally, 1969]). Authority is a prominent topic in writings on management and on administrative or managerial behavior. Relevant material turns up in the study of (behavioral, not normative) decision making and on the uses of experts as advisers (for a good example, see Irving L. Janis, *Victims of Groupthink* [Boston: Houghton Mifflin, 1972]). There ought to be abundant relevant material in the literature of education, but I am unfamiliar with that literature, as with the literature of theology, where authority is a major topic. Studies of public opinion, political behavior, cults and mass movements, mass media use, popular culture, and consumer behavior contribute relevant bits, as do any number of ethnographic studies of working-class or middle-class culture. This is what makes the bibliographical situation for the student of cognitive authority so taxing: hardly any area of study in the social sciences is without some relevance. When one adds the entire literature of history, randomly dotted with riches, one sees the hopelessness of attempting a complete bibliography of relevant literature.

A final word on epistemology. Although this book is no work of philosophical epistemology, there is a philosophical view of epistemology that I find particularly congenial: Richard Rorty's view of epistemological behaviorism, described in his *Philosophy and the Mirror of Nature* (Princeton: Princeton University Press, 1979), esp. pp. 173-82. Addressed to philosophers, the work is not easy reading for the layman. Rorty in effect denies any special authority to mainstream philosophy in questions of cognitive authority. (Cf. above, chapter 4, note 51.) The epistemological behaviorism that Rorty advocates, and for which he claims John Dewey and Ludwig Wittgenstein as adherents, appears to me to amount simply to the social study of knowledge, or social epistemology. Epistemological questions are social questions, and social epistemology is the only epistemology. This view can be expected to be found unattractive by professional philosophers but very attractive by those of us interested in the social study of knowledge.

INDEX